'Akira Mizubayashi is a man whose dog, Mélodie, taught him what it means to be human because she enabled him to discover his creatureliness in their companionship. It was a discovery that could be made only in the light of love, with patient attention. Mizubayashi reflects upon, and in the quality of his prose shows us by example, what literature can reveal about the truthful possibilities in our relations to fellow creatures who are not human beings.'

Raimond Gaita

MÉLODIE

MÉLODIE

a memoir of love and longing

AKIRA MIZUBAYASHI

Translated by Stephanie Anderson

MELBOURNE UNIVERSITY PRESS

MELBOURNE UNIVERSITY PRESS
An imprint of Melbourne University Publishing Limited
11–15 Argyle Place South, Carlton, Victoria 3053, Australia
mup-info@unimelb.edu.au
www.mup.com.au
First published 2016

French text © Akira Mizubayashi, 2016
English translation © Stephanie Anderson, 2016
Design and typography © Melbourne University Publishing Limited, 2016

This book is copyright. Apart from any use permitted under the *Copyright Act 1968* and subsequent amendments, no part may be reproduced, stored in a retrieval system or transmitted by any means or process whatsoever without the prior written permission of the publishers.

Every attempt has been made to locate the copyright holders for material quoted in this book. Any person or organisation that may have been overlooked or misattributed may contact the publisher.

Cover design by Mary Callahan
Text design and typesetting by Patrick Cannon
Printed in Australia by McPherson's Printing Group

National Library of Australia Cataloguing-in-Publication entry:

Mizubayashi, Akira, 1951– author.

Mélodie: a memoir of love and longing/Akira Mizubayashi; originally published in French; translated by Stephanie Anderson.

9780522869880 (paperback)
9780522869897 (ebook)

Mizubayashi, Akira, 1951–
Mélodie (Dog)
Dogs—Japan—Anecdotes.
Grief.

Other Creators/Contributors:
Anderson, Stephanie, translator.

843.92

In memory of Jiro Mizubayashi, my father

FOREWORD

A JAPANESE MAN I'd never met before approached me in front of Gallimard: 'You're the author of *The Difficulty of Being a Dog*! My dog has been dead for two years, and I dream about her every night.'

That was the beginning of our friendship. A friendship, I should add, between three of us under the aegis of our departed dogs: my Ulysse, J-B Pontalis's Oreste and Akira Mizubayashi's Mélodie.

Having published his fine homage to the French language, *A Language from Another Place*, Akira Mizubayashi felt the need to create, again in French, this evocation of his beloved golden retriever Mélodie, a poetic *tombeau* (tomb: an elegy), as it used to be called. Mélodie was in fact one of those to whom *A Language from Another Place* was dedicated.

As we read, tears will inevitably come to our eyes, more than once. Akira Mizubayashi knows not only how to move us, but also how to make us acknowledge somewhat paradoxical feelings. For example, the often-mentioned death of his father and the allusion to his ashes along with those of the animal. Or again, because of their high-spirited dance, two dogs are compared to Octavian and Sophie in *Der Rosenkavalier*. And Mizubayashi shares music, Mozart, with the aptly named Mélodie.

The narrative makes us aware, too, of the extent to which the habits of daily life are not the same in Tokyo and Paris. What does a Japanese dog do when, on returning home, you take off your shoes?

We are made conscious more than once that the author is a specialist of the eighteenth century. But his philosophy spans the thinkers of the Enlightenment to Kurosawa's *Seven Samurai*. We learn he is against Descartes (animal-machines) and Malebranche, but for Rousseau and even more so Montaigne. This book is a hymn to fidelity and still more a philosophical reflection on waiting. What better embodiment of waiting than a dog? The dog named Hachi who, every evening, waited for his master at the train station exit. But in vain because his master was dead. Hachi waited for ten years before he in turn was to die. Today he has his own bronze statue at Shibuya station.

Near the conclusion of this book in which memory speaks with no fear of flouting the rules of propriety, we shall come across Akira Mizubayashi walking in the footsteps of Henry James to erect in his turn an altar to the dead.

Roger Grenier

From the heart—may it go to the heart!

LUDWIG VAN BEETHOVEN, *Missa Solemnis*

Tereza kept stroking Karenin's head, which was quietly resting in her lap, while something like the following ran through her mind: There's no particular merit in being nice to one's fellow man. She had to treat the other villagers decently, because otherwise she couldn't live there. Even with Tomas, she was obliged to behave lovingly because she needed him. We can never establish with certainty what part of our relations with others is the result of our emotions—love, antipathy, charity or malice—and what part is predetermined by the constant power play among individuals.

True human goodness, in all its purity and freedom, can come to the fore only when its recipient has no power. Mankind's true moral test, its fundamental test (which lies deeply buried from view), consists of its attitude towards those who are at its mercy: animals. And in this respect mankind has suffered a fundamental débâcle, a débâcle so fundamental that all others stem from it.

MILAN KUNDERA, *The Unbearable Lightness of Being*
(TRANS. MICHAEL HENRY HEIM)

PRELUDE

1

A HOWL IN THE NIGHT

SOMETHING LIKE THE howl of a wolf, short and shrill, broke the silence and tore the man from his sleep. He gave a start and sat up. In the gloom he saw the head of the dog, watching him. She was lying on a bath towel at the foot of the big bed, while beside the sitting man, lay a woman, half awake, half asleep. The dog howled again so plaintively that the man thought she was crying out for help. He moved towards her, while she looked steadily at him. From outside, through a crack in the shutters, not entirely closed, there came a wan, washed-out light that lit up the upper half of the dog's head, revealing her age The man noticed that she was panting, when only a few minutes ago she had been lying peacefully in the soft warmth of the night.

'What's wrong, my friend?' the man asked. 'You're in pain? You want to tell me something?'

PRELUDE

She was holding out her right paw; the man took it. He rubbed his cheek against hers. Then he whispered in her ear, 'Let's get you lying next to me.'

Then, with a swift tug, he pulled the towel on which the dog lay motionless, her gaze still intently fixed on him, moving it two metres or so. She was now lying right in close to the man, like a frightened child nestling in its father's arms.

'Good night. Sleep well', said the man.

The dog stretched out. The man placed his hand on her swollen shoulder. Then he slid it gently, in the direction of the growth of her fur, right down her back. He repeated this several times, and the animal became calm again and her breathing regular. All the fear and agitation of the endless lonely night had gone; she seemed to surrender herself to the reassuring and soothing power of the feeling of not being alone and abandoned, to the tactile and olfactory sensation of this human presence, with her, here and now.

Finally, the man fell asleep, his right hand on the dog's neck, which, bulging strangely, felt worryingly vulnerable.

The next morning, on waking, he found himself in the same position: his hand still resting on the dog's relaxed body. She hadn't budged an inch either.

2

2 DECEMBER 2009

NIGHT WAS FALLING. At times you could hear the driving rain and the hysterical howling of the north wind.

She was tired, she'd become weak. It would soon be her mealtime, but she wasn't hungry. That morning she hadn't eaten anything. She wasn't thirsty either. Her front paws were as big as logs. Her tongue and her upper lip were completely white as if drained of blood. She had no strength left. She was out of breath even though she'd made no physical effort at all. Could she walk? No. Could she get up? Perhaps not. She was in too much pain. She was exhausted. Soon she would be lost, would disappear into the vast and shadowy silence of oblivion. What on earth was the time? When would he be coming home? It was Wednesday. It was the day he came home late, sometimes very late, after ten o'clock. What was he doing? Could she hang on until then?

PRELUDE

She was lying next to the big marital bed, her muzzle placed on the edge, without energy. Suddenly, using all her strength, she tried to get up again. No doubt she wanted to move nearer to the hall so that she could listen out for the merest sound of footsteps approaching. But she couldn't manage it. She waited for a few minutes. Then, she sat up on her haunches with a start as if she were waking up from a horrible nightmare. Her swollen front feet supported all of her weight. She sighed deeply.

A sharp pain was becoming more acute. It was tearing at her chest. Her sight was dimming. The lights were going out one by one. Then she picked up the faint sound of a door creaking, the cupboard door closing again. What? Was she going to leave? It wasn't possible ... Oh, please no, please no ... With an extraordinary effort she got up and began to walk, painfully ... She got to the living room, and she saw Michèle, who'd just put on her coat.

'What are you doing? Why did you get up? You should have called me! Are you thirsty? Do you want some water? ... Oh, you're ill. Yes, I know ... Don't force yourself. Go on, lie down here. And rest ... Yes, that's it. There you are. Is that better? You see, you'll feel better like that ... What's the matter? You look so sad! ... You don't want me to leave, is that it? But you know, I've only put my coat on to go out and get a few things. You don't want me to go away? Is that why you got up? To tell me not to go ... Is that it? Oh yes, that's what it is ...'

With a slightly hesitant movement as if she were lifting something heavy, the dog gave Michèle her swollen right paw. Michèle clasped it and then shook it tenderly, as a sign of affection.

'Yes, I understand now, I understand … Don't worry, I'm not leaving, I'm staying with you.'

It was exactly 5.37pm. It was raining. She seemed relieved, she relaxed and stretched out fully. Then she sighed. And after this long sigh there came faint death rattles.

The howling of the north wind could be heard more clearly now.

'Oh no, you're not going like that! You can't do that! No, come on, be brave! I'm going to call Mr D. He'll come straight away. And then you'll feel better … But you're ill, you're very ill, I can see that. I haven't heard you crying out in pain like this before. I can't bear it … I don't want to see you like this! What can I do for you, tell me, what can I do?'

While she dialled the vet's number she went on talking to her dog, not stopping, to give herself courage.

The dog was in dreadful, crushing, pain. She couldn't take it any longer. The world was growing darker. Very softly, from the upper part of her visual field, a grey curtain was coming down. She gave the woman sitting beside her a last look of tenderness, which conveyed a silent word whose meaning seemed obvious to her. Her eyes were moister than usual. In the dark silence of that first month of winter, shot through with strangled rattles, an unspeakable fear took hold. A scarcely audible woman's voice, coming from the cell phone left lying on the floor, said to leave a message …

'My God! No! No … no … NO!'

PRELUDE

The telephone rang.

'Hello?'

'Hello, it's me, the meeting's just finished, I'm coming home straight away. How's it going?'

Then silence, for a couple of seconds.

'No, it's … it's not good at all. She's getting weaker, you know … Get home quickly. But be careful on your bike. I don't know if it's still raining, but it's really windy tonight …'

'Yes, I'm leaving in a few minutes. See you soon.'

I was in a teeming crowd heading towards Y station. It wasn't raining very heavily. With the break in the weather people began closing their umbrellas. I closed mine. I hurried. I could only think of getting back to Mélodie as quickly as I could. I saw nothing, I heard nothing, I thought of nothing; I walked and walked. I walked so mechanically that in the middle of a pedestrian crossing I trod on the heel of the young woman just in front of me. She tripped, falling on to her knees.

'Oh, I'm sorry, forgive me.'

She got up straight away, while I picked up her upturned red shoe and gave it back to her. Embarrassed, she gave me a nice smile, which made me smile in return.

'I'm sorry, I was miles away. You're OK? Can you walk? Are you going to the station?'

'Yes.'

'Me too.'

We caught the same overcrowded train. There were two or three people between us: we weren't brave enough to start up a conversation. In a quarter of an hour we got to Nakano. I broke the silence.

2 DECEMBER 2009

'I'm getting out here.'

'Me too', she answered softly.

'Oh, so you live in Nakano too!'

We went down the stairs together. As soon as I'd gone through the ticket gate I said to her, 'Goodbye, and, again, my apologies.'

'No, don't apologise. It doesn't hurt anymore.' She smiled. She told me that she was going to take the bus. I replied that I was going to pick up my bike. We parted. She made me a little bow, and I bowed too, a little more deeply. She disappeared into a long queue that was waiting for the bus …

I made my way to the parking lot for bicycles and motorcycles. It started raining again. I didn't open my umbrella: it was too dangerous to ride with an open umbrella. The dark sky trapped between the highest buildings of the central part of the district whistled as the wind from the north blew through them. It was cold. I turned into the street where the town hall was, where there was never much traffic. I followed it down through the shopping district. I often stop there to buy books at the big bookshop. But that day I wanted to get home as fast as I could. I was driven by a growing sense of anxiety, an indefinable feeling of urgency. I arrived. I took the stairs four at a time. I slid the key into the lock and opened the door. I was soaked through. Michèle ran to me.

The house was dark. Baroque music was playing. The polyphony of the stringed instruments filled the air. Michèle kissed me, in tears.

'Mélodie is gone. She waited for you … But in the end she couldn't take it any longer.'

PRELUDE

I cross the dimly lit living room. The two sliding doors of the dining room are open. Mélodie's body is lying on a futon placed against the back wall. Her head is hidden by a big bunch of flowers in a round, brown vase. A little candle in the candle-holder in the shape of an old lamp creates a kind of yellow aura around her mortal remains. Covered over by a slightly faded orange towel, her body lies outstretched, the nerves and muscles peacefully letting go.

I come close and crouch down. I touch her head. It is warm. Fifteen years ago, when I touched the head of my father, who had been dead for six hours, it was freezing cold. I lift up the towel. An unfamiliar smell wafts up. I stroke Mélodie's inanimate body, which still looks like the one I took in my arms this morning. I am struck by a vague sensation of warmth. It is a body half alive, already in the realm of shadows, but still quivering with the vestiges of life, ebbing away like the sea at low tide. It is resisting the relentless invasion of the cold.

The rain gets heavier again. The wind rages more strongly.

The Baroque music, Albinoni or Tartini, is still playing. Her eyes are not like they were before. They were black, big, tender, overflowing with warmth and affection. Now they are grey, small. They no longer look at me. They are lost in the emptiness. Suddenly, an abyss has been carved out between us. My voice can no longer reach her ears. It is lost in the cold, pronounced grey of her pupils.

I lie down on the wooden floor next to the futon to be as close to her as possible. With my head against her head,

2 DECEMBER 2009

my nose against her nose, I look into her dull eyes, which bear the trace of utter exhaustion. I put my right hand on her neck, on her nose, then on her upper lip, breathing the last vestiges of her breath. My field of vision is entirely filled by her head. I plunge deeper into the well of her eyes. There is a huge grey circle lit by the candle. I am in a cypress forest at nightfall. Or am I at the entrance to a tunnel at sunset, a time tunnel, a corridor opening to take me far into time and space?

Diary Extract 1

Fragments that Have Slipped from the Notebook of a Dog's Companion

I wonder what images will appear on the screen of my dark inner cinema at the moment of my death. My father died some time during the night of 2 April 1994, alone, far from any familial or familiar presence, in a ward of several beds in a small private hospital of a town named Stork River. He had just been put into hospital. The coming of the Grim Reaper is always sudden. We had prepared ourselves, but we weren't ready.

In *Literature or Life*, Jorge Semprún devotes several pages of shattering beauty to the death agony of the great sociologist Maurice Halbwachs in the Buchenwald concentration camp. The Spanish writer notes that, 'conscious of the need for a prayer', he recited aloud, for the one who 'was slowly being emptied of his vital substance', some lines from Baudelaire: "'O death, old captain, it is time, let us weigh anchor! … Our hearts known to you are filled with beams of light!'" 'A slight quiver' then appeared 'on the lips' of his old teacher. I would have liked to do the same for my father, who lay snugly in a hospital bed. I am not ashamed to say it. I am not Semprún; my father is not Halbwachs; our circumstances are not tragic like theirs. But the need—it is imperative—to say a prayer and to be with the one who is making this decisive leap is the same.

My father passed away in the nocturnal silence of a hospital ward. No one knew of his dying, apart perhaps from the person in the next bed, who would have noticed some irregularity in his breathing.

I imagine in vain the thoughts that would have crossed his mind; in vain I picture the familial scenes of times past which he might have replayed in his mind's eye like a kaleidoscope of images. I remain forever separated from the truth that was lost to silence and ink-black darkness. What do you see when death comes to you? What happens at the moment when consciousness falls into the abyss of nothingness? All the dead know it; the living remain ignorant.

Part I

TO BE SENSITIVE, TO BE COMPASSIONATE

3

A DOUBLE BIRTH

IT'S SUMMER. During the day the heat is oppressive, and sometimes it goes on into the night. But on this particular morning we wake up and it is unexpectedly cool. How delightful! So I get up and go for a walk. I like to steal along the peaceful streets of the sleeping town. I do a big loop of the neighbourhood, often walking by the memorial garden of Hyakkannon (Hundred Statuettes of the Merciful Goddess). There are trees there, cherries and maples. I pass people walking dogs who meet in the middle of the street or beneath a maple still covered in greenery to stop and chat for a moment. I run, I stop. I run again. An hour later I return, dripping with sweat. A warm shower revives me.

A friend calls us around two in the afternoon to tell us that her golden retriever, oddly named Danna—oddly because it's a Japanese name meaning 'Master, head of the house'—has just given birth to eight puppies. She knows that my daughter,

TO BE SENSITIVE, TO BE COMPASSIONATE

Julia-Madoka, who has just turned twelve, has been longing to have a puppy for ages. She tells me that she'll invite us to come and see them when the puppies have grown a little and are ready to leave their mother and the house where they were born.

Two months later we are in the apartment of Mr and Mrs G, where Danna and her puppies are entertaining a large gathering. A square space, the equivalent of two tatami mats, fenced with flattened cardboard boxes, serves as the puppies' house, and it's there that, night and day, the mother feeds them and raises them with unflagging devotion. Two or three puppies are having fun biting and fighting while the others nap. Among those who are awake, the most active one turns its head and notices that three heads have appeared above the very high cardboard wall. It looks at the marvelling face of the schoolgirl who looks back at it. A meeting has taken place. Someone catches the puppy and takes it up out of the house as if they were carrying it by helicopter. Now it is placed on the lap of the schoolgirl who a few minutes before had gazed at it in rapt attention.

The puppy has fallen asleep. It has been on her little lap for a good hour, without moving a muscle.

Night is softly falling.

Our apartment isn't far from Mr and Mrs G's. Ten minutes' walk at the most. But the puppy is too heavy for the twelve-year-old schoolgirl to carry.

'Dad will carry it.'

She tries to resist but very quickly gives in. It really is heavy. The puppy would be happy to skip along, but it isn't allowed to walk for the moment; any contact with the ground has to be avoided, as it is swarming with hundreds of different kinds of microbes that are harmful to new puppies not yet vaccinated.

We get to the house. I put the puppy in the hall on the wooden floor. It moves shyly towards the living room. The radio is on; the puppy is greeted by a passage from Mozart's Piano Concerto No. 9, known as *Jeunehomme*. It stops for a moment. It looks all around. The scenery is new, made up of indoor plants, some prints and a number of wooden shelves on which are placed, vertically or horizontally, numerous bound sheets of paper. It squats for a moment and continues on.

A little pool of yellowish liquid has formed.

The puppy continues this first exploration of its new environment. It goes into a smaller room where it looks up at a big oval-shaped board held up by four posts. It passes through some wooden uprights—not as tall as the four posts—which, grouped in fours, hold up a little wicker square placed across them. When it has emerged from this makeshift shelter it notices a big mattress covered with a brand-new orange towel. It gets onto it and lies down. It seems to have understood instinctively that this was to be its spot. It rests its muzzle on its front paws and gives a sigh.

Night comes. The lights go on in the city. The throbbing of the old air conditioners stops. The schoolgirl, who had consulted several books about dog training when she dreamt of having a dog, has placed the little animal on an absorbent napkin three times in the space of two hours, and each time it has produced a few drops. It seems to have understood that it wasn't to go just anywhere, but only on this white nappy, which, with its three yellow stains, now looks like an old, faded map of the world.

It is sleeping now, its body in a state of complete and utter relaxation; it breathes as peacefully as can be, far from the noise of cars and far from men's shouting, but far, too, from its mother's warm breath, silent and comforting.

'We'll leave her like that. You go to bed now too.'

'Yes, thank you, Dad, thank you, Mum.'

'Don't worry about her, my darling. Good night then.'

We are all whispering.

We are present, in a state of wonder, at a birth.

4

THE PAIN OF THE FIRST NIGHT

I CLOSE MY EYES. Behind my eyelids images of the day that has just passed follow one after the other. But, little by little, they recede like the waves of a calm sea, drawing me down into the silence and oblivion of my night, just beginning. Just when my consciousness flickers and begins to sink fully into the dark depths, a weak little moan crosses the length of the living room, which separates me from the room occupied by the new inhabitant. I get up and go towards the moans, which are becoming more frequent and intensifying. I turn on the little lamp on the writing desk.

'What's the matter, little one? You're sad to be separated from your mum and your brothers and sisters? Is that it? Yes, that's quite normal. It's your first big night alone. You really have to get used to it …'

She is sitting up and looks at me imploringly. My eyelids are heavy with sleep, and I just want to close them again.

I crouch down: my eyes are exactly level with hers. We look at each other. She lifts her right paw—it's so small—and waves it in the air, but she isn't able to put it anywhere.

'You have to go to sleep now. It's getting late. Everyone's in bed. And you need to go to bed too. Tomorrow, everything will be OK. Don't you think?'

While I'm talking to her I almost fall asleep again. I take the little golden-coated dog in my arms; I feel some resistance, as if she doesn't want to be held prisoner in my embrace. I get up again and go out of the dining room. Already I hear plaintive little whistling noises, and I think I know what they mean: 'Don't leave me by myself. Stay here with me.' The sobbing of this little creature, so abruptly severed from the sacred bond that tied her to the world, persuades me to stay with her.

I go and get my overcoat, put it on and sit down on the mattress beside her, propping myself against the wall. So she lies down; without the slightest hesitation she puts her head on my lap and immediately drifts off into the deepest of sleeps. As for me, I sleep without sleeping. Waking after a time, aching and stiff, I look at my watch: 3.27am. I feel the discomfort in my neck and buttocks especially. She hasn't moved an inch. I put my hand on her head. I hear the light snoring of a child who, completely trusting, gives herself up to the deep silence of the night.

I drop off to sleep again and become submerged in a dream in which a pure-white puppy is racing wildly through a huge forest of bamboo.

5

FIRST MEAL

THE MOMENT WE decided to bring a dog into our home, one of Danna's litter, her name came to us. This was a house of music, imbued with chords and rhythms, and it was only natural that the little dog's name should chime harmoniously with music.

She opens her eyes, quite amazed to be there on her mattress. Was she dreaming of being nestled against the soft, wavy white fur of her mother? She gets up and stretches, quivering all over.

'She's just woken up', whispers my daughter.

I come into the dining room. Our eyes meet, hers revealing how very anxious she is. It's as if she is asking me a question. A front paw is in the air. With her head tilted to one side, all her attention is focused on me, as if to decipher my expression and my gestures; as if not the slightest of movements will go unnoticed. I would never have imagined that the gaze of a puppy could be as eloquent and interrogating as this.

TO BE SENSITIVE, TO BE COMPASSIONATE

I prepare her first meal. A mug of kibble in a pure white bowl. She is sitting there, very well-behaved. How and why has she understood that she is not to leap on her food? I don't know. In a firm and serious tone I had simply said, 'No!' just as she was about to throw herself at her little meal.

Almost imperceptibly, the anxiety she showed by tilting her head just slightly is there in the impatient look she now gives me. Authoritative, I give her the command '*Yoshi!* (Go on!)'.

She gets lightly to her feet and puts her muzzle right into the heap of kibble. In a couple of minutes it is all gone. She looks at me again as if she wants something else. The schoolgirl, observing the whole scene, makes a suggestion: 'What about some water?'

'Yes, good idea.'

I take a hollow earthenware dish, fill it with water and place it beside the bowl. Her eyes follow my every move. She goes towards the dish and leans over it until she is just brushing the reflecting surface of the water. She sees herself in it, like Narcissus, and is no doubt amazed to see a being that looks like her. She says hello to it, kindly extending her right paw towards the other. The mirror cracks, droplets spatter; she steps back a pace.

Some moments later a shy little lapping can be heard, a delightful tinkling of water. She gives me a look of contentment. Drops fall from her jaws and sprinkle the floor, beside her wet white paw.

6

WAITING FOR THE FIRST OUTING

THE DAYS PASSED. October flew by. November was colder and rainier than in previous years. The maple leaves turned red; those of the cherries turned bright orange; those of the gingko turned yellow. Then they fell one by one, blown away by the north wind. When the first days of December finally came, dry and filled with light, the bare trees were like great statues, standing there with a haughty air, more vigorous than ever; their outspread, muscular branches seemed to assert that they no longer needed outer garments in flaming hues.

Danna's offspring was growing up. When we looked at the photos we'd taken when she'd first come to us, we realised that the life of a dog was thrown into an accelerated developmental process quite unlike that of human beings. The period of confinement after the vaccinations was coming to an end. The schoolgirl was impatient to see her dog quite free to run about in the street. Her parents, for their part, were patiently awaiting the first outing. The space available to Mélodie, that of our apartment, which was by no means minuscule, was no longer anything like the area needed by a dog in full and vigorous growth, for its never tiring body to expend its energy. Once a day, as night was falling, the whole habitable surface of the apartment was transformed into an athletics field; the pure-white juvenile body, sometimes coloured scarlet red by the last rays that came in through the skylight, would run at full speed, doing two or three circuits of the apartment. After that she emptied her bowl, always in a well-mannered way.

The day often finished with the sudden visit of the Sandman. She was afraid of nothing. Our house was her house. She seemed to have moulded as serenely and naturally as can be into the very shape of our existence. Sometimes she would sleep under the kitchen table, her tummy in the air, in a state of fearless surrender, her nerves completely relaxed, her whole body in a wonderfully trusting state of letting go.

7

FIRST OUTING

THE DAY OF the much anticipated first outing finally came. Everything was ready: a little yellow collar, a red leash made of rope, a little walks bag in which there was a bottle of water, a brush and a pile of coloured advertising liftouts, carefully folded in four. She was alert to the unusual sense of agitation that ran through every room of the house. She sat in the front hallway. Her eyes followed each of us as we went from room to room, intrigued. She'd never seen such hurrying on the part of the co-occupants of the familial space.

I picked up the car keys. I put her collar around her neck, I attached the leash, I picked up the little bag, and finally I opened the door. She leapt up in spite of the force—mine—that restrained her. I shouted her name. She calmed down at once and followed me obediently, slowly down the stairs towards the car park. She hesitated at the open door of our old Accord. She didn't know what to do. I helped her up onto the back seat. She resisted, but once in the car she lay down as if that's what she'd always done. I in turn sat in the car, and we waited for my wife and my daughter.

We headed towards Akiruno, a municipality in the western suburbs of Tokyo, fifty kilometres from where we lived. Lying between the mother, who kept up a constant stream of praise for her good manners, and the teenage girl, who kept stroking her head, Mélodie remained placid and imperturbably motionless during this baptism in car travel. And a few minutes later, helped by the dull vibration of the engine, she fell into a slumber that lasted until we reached the end of our journey.

Akiruno was where the A family, who had taken another of Danna's offspring, which they named Octave, lived. The purpose of the first outing was to bring about a meeting between the brother and sister two months after they'd left the maternal fold. Greetings exchanged, we decided to go together to a big park a few hundred metres away. We walked tranquilly along a narrow street edged with clumps of azaleas and rhododendrons, which promised a bewitching display for spring. Danna's two puppies quickened their steps. When we arrived at the park we were amazed to find it deserted. It was a Sunday. It was almost three o'clock in the afternoon. No children in the sandpit, no old men on the benches positioned in the four corners of the park. Was everyone still at lunch, relaxed and carefree in a Sunday mood? The swings did not stir; the slide stood there like a little, bored giant. The sky smiled kindly on the two creatures finally released from their period of domestic imprisonment: just lightly hazy and free from the caprices of the wind, the light it sent them was filtered, soft, beneficent. I took off Mélodie's leash; Mrs A did the same with her dog.

Once liberated, the brother and sister presented us with a wondrous display. In one bound Mélodie propelled herself forward like a wild animal seizing its prey and began running with all her might. But after a few seconds she abruptly changed direction; elastically twisting her svelte body, she jumped to the left. Then, with a thrust that carried her high into the air, she caught sight of something that looked like a feather. She turned her head even further to the left before falling back to earth, and once her four paws were set on the sandy ground she rushed to chase the hairy object. Hell-bent on catching it, she pivoted frenetically, round and round, for several seconds. At last she collapsed in a heap, the tip of her tail in her mouth. Octave, who had taken off at the same time as his sister, ran towards her and, without meaning to, hit her full on. She was knocked over, but she got straight back up again and ran full pelt towards the end of the park. Octave, unperturbed by his sister's remarkable agility, immediately sped off, not wanting to be left too far behind. It was an extraordinary spectacle in which the brother and sister, with the vitality and impetuousness of full-blown adolescents, were engaged in a furious, reckless race, seemingly unstoppable. The two bodies passed first under a big hundred-year-old cherry tree denuded of its cloak of foliage, but that still shed shade with its majestically twisted branches. They were like two shooting stars in the dark sky, two silver rockets, one pursuing the other at dizzying speed. It was like watching a science fiction film in which spacecraft, like beams of white light, flashing and flying, surf over the blackness and finally slip away, swallowed up into the mysterious, far-flung reaches of the universe. They disappeared behind the shrubbery only to reappear instantly in the bright luminosity of the open space. The gap between the two bodies remained unchanged. At last they arrived at the swings, an area surrounded by an iron safety railing. Quick and nimble, Mélodie hurdled the first fence, without lessening her momentum or her driving strength, which were at their absolute peak, while her little brother followed, jumping five centimetres higher than the fence, with his four paws tucked carefully and neatly into the middle of his flat stomach. The benches and the monkey bars suddenly sprang up in front of them like policemen blocking the way. But they deftly avoided them and continued their feverish stampede. They passed behind the sandpit and dodged the little giant. When Mélodie had gone right around the path like this she stopped suddenly and, having taken a few steps sniffing I don't know what lying on the ground, she lay down and looked around her like a she-wolf whose gaze travels far, anxious to protect her cubs from potential enemies; or a general perhaps, surveying from the top of a hill his battalion lined up below him. As for Octave, he slowed his pace seeing that his sister didn't want to go round the park a second time. He retraced his steps; he placed himself delicately beside her and collapsed in a heap as though he'd used every last bit of energy. Then they stayed looking at each other for a long while. Their muzzles, pointed skywards, almost touched. Their big black eyes closed to form a thin thread,

Buddha-like, a sign of their happiness at being together in the gentle sunlight of a December afternoon.

But, a few moments later, the little brother got up again and went nonchalantly to the middle of the park. Immediately, Mélodie followed him. The contest we then witnessed was a magnificent performance. First Mélodie charged into Octave, the violent blow knocking him over. She leapt on him, nibbled his neck, his ears and his muzzle, at the same time sending him into a spiral of somersaults. When they'd covered three metres of ground as a spinning golden ball, they stood up and launched into improvising a new kind of folk dance, standing on their back legs, supporting each other, hugging and murmuring to each other in joyful little squeals, 'This is so good, we're so happy!' Then they returned to their wild tumbling as if performing elegant dance steps had never held any attraction for them.

Like this, in a succession of frolicking, somersaulting, whirling and enchanting rhythmic movements, a good ten minutes passed at the end of which they collapsed in complete exhaustion. Fatigue overcame the desire to carry on the festivities. They were utterly spent. All at once the tenseness in their muscles relaxed; the two dogs collapsed. At last they lay outstretched and did not move. The only sound was their deep and rapid breathing. We could see their stomachs rising and falling in a wildly accelerated rhythm, which, little by little, became regular again.

The sun was already going down; sometimes it slipped behind the clouds. Slowly, very slowly, the day gave way to night, longer, more soothing, filled with first dreams, first enchanted memories.

/ 8

ARDENT YOUTH

THAT NIGHT MÉLODIE slept straight through from 7.45pm to 7.10 in the morning. Fatigue had plunged her down into the very depths of the well of sleep. When she woke up, an amazing thing had happened: she was no longer a giddy young girl. From one day to the next she stopped chewing the skirting boards and the chair legs. A whole world, a whole epoch, lay far behind her. In a night she had acquired a degree of maturity. Between the ancient history of childhood and already waning adolescence on the one hand and, on the other, an inexorably rapidly encroaching future, there opened out, as if by a miracle, a time that was immobile, infinitely precarious and fragile, in which ardent youth came fully into its own.

Michèle and Julia-Madoka had gone to bed. I settled myself in the living room, on the sofa. I closed my eyes. My mind's eye was filled by this one image, that of the two dogs celebrating their keen impatience to live, tasting their inexpressible joy at being together, exalting in their pure pleasure in being alive and spreading their wings to revel in boundless play. I saw in them the expression of ardent youth affirming itself with all its might in the passionate urgency of a present that goes on forever. I was delighting in the happiness of having been witness to theirs. I didn't want to sleep. I wanted to go on experiencing the intoxicating effect of transgressive youth. I didn't want to let the beautiful rose, picked in all its freshness, die, or the fire that was blazing go out or the vital energy gathered up in this privileged instant be used up and destroyed. No, what I wanted was for the sweet imprint of this radiant afternoon to become part of me. I wanted to preserve its quivering trace, the wonder and the mystery.

Suddenly, I don't know why, I thought of the young couple in *Der Rosenkavalier* by Richard Strauss. And deep in my ears there reverberated the music of the beginning of the second act of this opera that I was at the time discovering in the wake of *The Marriage of Figaro*. It was an urgent, unstoppable appeal. An outpouring, a deluge, as sudden as it was strange. In listening to this enchanting music I could materialise and prolong the memory of a Mélodie in the full bloom of her youth, for it seemed to me to respond quite perfectly and wonderfully to the image of these two living beings who were non-human but who could still delight in their present happiness before being thrust into the uncertain future of their short lives.

It was getting late, but I wanted to immerse myself in the magic of Strauss's music. I turned on the DVD player and I watched the whole scene in which Octavian and Sophie meet for the first time over a silver rose. It is passed from one hand to the other and the two characters, whose youthful desire is expressed by a wonderful interplay of two feminine voices, breathe in 'a drop of Persian attar' that is contained in it. They remain as if frozen in an emotion at once peaceful and overwhelming that can only be called love.

Diary Extract 2

**Fragments that Have Slipped from
the Notebook of a Dog's Companion**

The story of *Der Rosenkavalier* comes to us as a full narrative development of the couple formed by the countess and Cherubino in *The Marriage of Figaro*. Hofmannsthal and Strauss take up the narrative of *Figaro* just when the little page addresses to the lady he loves the song beginning 'You who know what love is ...' to imagine a different development of the scenario Da Ponte had conceived. In *Der Rosenkavalier* the love barely hinted at between the countess and Cherubino becomes the centre of the drama lived out by the Marschallin and Octavian. Despite all the differences that separate their work from the Mozart model, Hofmannsthal and Strauss make repeated references to *Figaro*: the disparity of age between Octavian and the Marschallin, between he who is no longer really an adolescent but not fully an adult and she whose status is that of the 'woman of thirty' abandoned by her husband; the succession of disguises of the young nobleman, the Don Juan-like figure of Ochs, who

TO BE SENSITIVE, TO BE COMPASSIONATE

must give up Sophie as Almaviva must give up Suzanne ... That said, *Der Rosenkavalier*, in contrast to *The Marriage of Figaro*, doesn't celebrate the birth of any kind of happy community. What is honoured is just the union of a fairly dissolute boy whose parents are of the nobility and a girl whose parents are of the bourgeoisie, and victim of an oppressive upbringing. The interest of this work of Strauss's therefore resides elsewhere.

What strikes me in *Der Rosenkavalier* is, dare I say it, the philosophical dimension of the work: the meditation of the Marschallin on aging, on time's destructive work, is a crucial moment. As we see when, towards the end of the first act, the great noblewoman sings:

> One would say that today I must feel the fragility of all ephemeral things, right to the bottom of my heart; learn that one must not wish to keep hold of anything, that one's arms close around emptiness, that everything slips through our fingers, how everything comes loose when one thinks one holds it close, how everything dissipates, like dreams and mist ... Time is a strange thing. Living day to day, it means nothing to us. But suddenly it is all we feel. It is around us. It is also in us. It streams down our mirrors, it drips from my temples. Between me and you on it flows, noiselessly, like sand in an hourglass.

What I find so marvellous in the context of this melancholy meditation on the passage of time is that, right in the middle of the work, at the very beginning of the second act, Strauss has given us an in-between state—a kind of 'true youth of the world' to use the beautiful expression that we find in Rousseau's *Second Discourse*—already removed from the time of the Marschallin (which is noble) but not yet subject to that of Sophie (which is bourgeois), in a truly

DIARY EXTRACT 2

miraculous meeting that brings together, by means of a perfumed silver rose, two young people who desire each other:

> SOPHIE: … It has a strange perfume. Like roses—like a real rose.
>
> OCTAVIAN: Yes, a drop of Persian attar has been placed in it.
>
> SOPHIE: One might say it was a celestial rose, not like those in our gardens, a rose of holy Paradise. Don't you think so? (Octavian leans over the rose she is holding out to him, then he rises and his gaze is fixed on Sophie's mouth.) It is like a heavenly greeting. Already, too strong to be borne. It draws you, as if bonds tightened around your heart. (in a soft voice) Where then could I have experienced such rapture?
>
> OCTAVIAN: (at the same time, as if unaware of Sophie's presence, in an even softer voice) Where could I have experienced such rapture?
>
> SOPHIE: I must find this blessed place! Even if I were to die on the way! But I shall not die. It is far off yet. Time, eternity, merge together in this sublime moment; I shall not forget it until I die.
>
> OCTAVIAN: (at the same time) I was a child, I did not yet know her. Who am I then? How did I come to her? How did she come to me? If I were not a man, I would swoon. What a sublime moment; I shall not forget it until I die.

This is a scene of sublime beauty, one that takes the breath away. And the word sublime is of course spoken by the two characters. Can one remain indifferent to such a profusion of light, to such an outpouring of happiness? Is it possible not to be profoundly moved, body and soul, by such an impression of happy inertia, of slowness ascending? It is a moment of eternity crystallised, a fragment of paradise which we are allowed to glimpse, an angel's descent to Earth, the implanting and propagation of the ever and always in the fleeting instant. To see and hear Anne Sofie von Otter (Octavian) and Barbara Bonney (Sophie), conducted by Carlos Kleiber, sing and live this extraordinary suspension of time is a disturbing experience, which makes one want to believe in absolute fidelity and in the unchangeableness of feeling.

Listening to the duet of Octavian and Sophie, dazzling in its revelation of a certain truth of youth, I saw again, through the profuse succession of images of my own vanished youth, the exuberant dance of the two dogs, drunk with their freedom and their immense youthful strength, without a hint of anxiety or any thought of the future.

9

TO UNDERSTAND

DAYS PASSED BY harmoniously; night followed peaceful night. Learning prodigiously quickly what not to do to make life not only possible but also pleasant, Mélodie acquired an exemplary sense of good behaviour and a tact that no one could have imagined. She never barked for no reason; she never destroyed things: not books, shoes, furniture, cushions, photo albums, knick-knacks, nothing in fact that constituted the domestic landscape was at risk; she never jumped on to our bed, or on to the yellow sofa in the living room; she never tried to take food that wasn't meant for her. Silent, discreet, almost retiring, she was there, like a filmy shadow. A sounding box too: her presence made us aware of our own breathing and, when we were moved by something, of the barely perceptible tremors of our hearts.

In the evenings, happy or unhappy about our work day, when my wife and I were waiting until it was time to go to bed, she would invariably place herself between us. When my daughter was enjoying giving me a demonstrative cuddle, she couldn't bear to be outside the circle of affection, in the intimacy of its embrace; she came up to me, pushed her rival away and lavished me with licks. She wanted to join with us, to be one of us, to be an integral part of the family clan: as soon as the three of us made ourselves comfortable on the sofa she would slide between us quite naturally, most often with her muzzle placed on my lap, to listen to us, to hear us talking about our concerns, our worries and, perhaps more rarely, what amused us. Did she understand what we were saying? I don't know. That obviously depends on the meaning we give to 'to understand'. She was really *with* us. The desire to be as close to us as she could, to be glued to us, was the message she gave us with the whole of her outstretched body and all of her communicative outpouring. What is 'to understand' if not the ability to listen for, and to be in unison with, what other people are feeling and thinking?

Mélodie understood us. Our hearts opened to hers; her heart responded to ours. At times I had the impression that she even read what was in them.

10

FIRST SEPARATION

SUMMER ARRIVED. Mélodie had grown up. She had blossomed and her stature was that of a fully grown adult. Her body was far better proportioned than those of men and women trapped by their daily fatigue and victims of the excesses in which they indulge of their own free will and that they try to offset somehow by strategies as costly as they are sophisticated; svelte, muscular and vigorous, her body now resembled an athlete's, radiating good health.

We planned to go to France to be with friends and family. I felt the desire to immerse myself again in the French language as well as in the web of ties that using it has spun for me. The problem, though, was our friend. To take her with us was inconceivable: the steps you had to go through, which were long and onerous, were a disincentive. Besides, we couldn't bear the idea of making her travel in the hold, where she would be subject to the noisy vibrations of the aircraft for the twelve-hour flight from Tokyo to Paris. So we decided to entrust her to the A family, whom she knew. She would have fun leading something of the country life, together with her brother, Octave. She would play tag with him. She would run madly through the fields; she would immerse herself gladly on steamy afternoons in the Akikawa River; perhaps, weaving through the thick undergrowth, she would imagine herself in the old dream of her ancestors; she would roll in the dirt just for the pleasure of rolling in the dirt.

Two days before our departure I took it upon myself to take her to Akiruno. First I put all of her things into a big bag. When everything was ready and I'd finally picked up the car keys, she guessed what was happening. She began to moan. Perhaps she felt torn between the desire to go with me and the desire to stay, not to leave her usual environment. In the end she decided to get into the car. Despite herself, clearly, because she didn't like the car. Throughout the whole journey she rested her head on the armrest between the two front seats; all the while I could feel her tranquil presence, made palpable by her regular breathing.

She was greeted by Octave in a warm and brotherly way. After an explosive few seconds of celebratory hugs the brother and sister took themselves off into an alcove that served as a kennel. It connected with the living room, which had a French door. Through the door I could see them moving around as I sat at the table talking with Mr and Mrs A, a cup of tea in my hand. A sweet fragrance of brown rice mixed with the green tea powder wafted around us.

I stayed chatting for a good hour. We talked especially about the difficult way of life that human society inflicted on the canine species, about all the explicit and implicit prohibitions imposed upon it, and finally about the scandalous irresponsibility towards it of some humans who only act in accordance with their immediate self-interest. For all this time Mélodie fixed me with her gaze, sitting in a pose of remarkable stillness. Now that the joy of meeting up with Octave had passed, was she anxious about what lay in store for her? No doubt she was.

I got up, bowed to Mr and Mrs A and said goodbye to them; I took the wheel and I drove off like a criminal who wants to get away from the scene of the crime as fast as he can. It was really an admission that I was guilty of abandoning her in a house that wasn't her own. I felt shot through with the piercing looks that she was sure to be casting at my back.

Five weeks later we returned to Tokyo; I was impatient to see her again. I knew that she'd moaned for two or three nights at the beginning of the holiday she'd spent apart from us. Was she well? What expression would she have on her face when she saw me again? Would she want to leave again with me?

Our Accord stops in front of our friends' house. Without waiting for us to appear, deep, resonant barks can be heard. We open the front gate. Mélodie's head, and Octave's, burst from the dark alcove. She climbs the fence, which is much higher than the garden hedge. We hear the strident and painful sound of claws raking the wooden fence. She succeeds, somehow, in getting over it and charges towards me. Propelled by an impulsive run-up, her body planes a metre above the ground. Anyone who didn't know her would be quite terrified by this frontal assault. As for me, I am delighted to be assailed by this rocket of blonde flesh. My hands grab hold of her front paws; in the region of my elbows I feel a burning sensation, which tears my skin like the stab of a dagger or the violent prick of a large needle.

'Hello, my friend. How are you? Oh yes, yes, you're so happy! Aren't you? You're just so happy!' The intense brevity of the greeting showed the length of the absence endured. In a few minutes my shapeless tee shirt, chosen in anticipation of a madly joyful reunion, was covered with muddy paw prints. My trousers, old ones that I only wore when I had work to do that would make my clothes dirty, were pierced in places by the repeated scratches from her protruding dewclaws.

When she'd satisfied her need to be effusive, she stood on her four feet. I crouched down, taking her by the neck. We were now facing each other. She licked my face from top to bottom as if she urgently had to express her feelings, driven by an irresistible need to pour out this overflowing affection. Suddenly I was struck by the sight of a streak of blood on both my forearms.

Mrs A offered to disinfect the wounds. I had to clench my teeth while she mercilessly rubbed them with alcohol-soaked cotton. The culprit for her part never took her eyes off me, looking through the French door of the living room and sitting up on her bottom in a state of anxious immobility similar to the one I'd observed five weeks earlier.

Night began to fall. The first signs of autumn could be heard in the incessant quivering of the leaves. In the garden a scattering of figs had now ripened. Nothing seemed to be hurrying us to leave behind this feeling of wellbeing ... But we had to bring ourselves to leave.

'Let's go home, my friend', I cried.

'Come on then, we're going', said Michèle.

In a flash she'd positioned herself in front of the car door. Her whole body was trembling, and she seemed to be making a point of saying that she was definitely coming with us. I didn't have to tell her what to do: she jumped in straight away and lay down. And she didn't move again until we reached our house.

That night Mélodie couldn't bear being on her own; she wouldn't let us leave her by herself on her mattress. She didn't stop howling until I gave in and finally opened the door of our bedroom. She came and settled herself in our intimate space as if it were the most natural thing in the world. She dug in at the foot of our bed and didn't budge from there. From that time on she abandoned her mattress at night.

All the world's nights are not the same, but after that it was there that hers, invariably, would be repeated. There were, however, two exceptions: the two weeks that were a little out of the ordinary that I shall recount presently and the two days before her great journey. During these two episodes, which were different in length but equally intense, she wanted to lie alongside me, close to me, to nestle right into me.

11

THE PUPPIES

SHE TURNED FOUR in August 2001. At once discreet and demonstrative, she had become a soothing presence; the energy she provided was healthy, invigorating and restorative. She was always there, with me, next to me, between us, among us. Imperturbably herself, she was like a mysterious barometer of the family atmosphere, of what each of us carried within us and brought back from the world around us, be it precious or pitiful. She'd become more than a companion, more than a friend, a being who could make us ill with worry, a creature for whom a word like *animal* or *beast* was not suitable, or tolerable, those terms too often being associated with the contempt that we express for human beings who are depraved and noxious and indeed infinitely more harmful to the general harmony of the world of human and non-human living beings than the animals and the beasts themselves. She was like a child resulting from an act of love, from the passionate lovemaking performed by my wife and me in our desire to bring a child into the world. She *was* my daughter, a daughter incarnated in a dog, whom I had had—in a fabulous story of some unknown civilisation—from intercourse with my wife while we were both changed into dogs. Among billions of possible dogs, it was she who'd been given to me—this is something of a miracle, as miraculous as the birth of a child, the fruit of a unique encounter, of that one night, that long night, of a man and a woman who make love.

One day I learnt of the death of one of Danna's offspring from the same litter. It had been taken by an illness of a violent nature that the vet had been unable to explain. It had vomited to the point of exhaustion and nothing had been able to stop this hellish reflex from taking hold of its body. I realised that dogs do not live as long as humans; my daughter was therefore aging six or seven times faster than I was. It was a scandalous situation. Of course the gap between the canine species and our own as to life expectancy constituted a basic fact dictated by the laws of nature, but I couldn't come to accept it.

So the idea came to me to perpetuate her life by asking her to leave descendants. We had a lot of trouble finding her a good match. But, finally, a suitor presented himself; the union took place at his house. And, one December day, she brought nine puppies into the world, one of which was stillborn.

To whelp—I cannot get used to this expression which seems to be inelegant, even ugly: why does French make a strict distinction between the act of giving birth to an offspring in the case of animals and the act of bringing a child into the world in the case of humans? The whelping, then, began towards midnight. We had asked for the assistance of Mrs A, who was the person closest to Mélodie outside my little family. She is a masseuse by profession, and quite familiar with what to do in this situation. She had already worked as a midwife, if I can put it like that, when Danna had given birth to her puppies four years earlier. As for me, an excruciating herniated disc condemning me to immobility, I was as useless as a folding umbrella in a raging typhoon.

An area equivalent to two tatamis fenced with sturdy cardboard had been prepared to serve as a delivery room. The mother-to-be was lying on old newspaper that had been spread out in readiness for the first contractions. Mrs A, seated facing Mélodie, placed her hands on her round belly. Each time that she stroked them right along her body from the neck to the rump Mélodie closed her eyes and, a few seconds later, stared at the masseuse with a gentle, pleading expression in her eyes.

The first one, dark brown, showed no delay in arriving. It was wrapped in a kind of gelatinous, translucent membrane, which the young mother tore and removed by licking it vigorously. This gesture was essential. The puppy would otherwise have been unable to breathe as it changed from one mode of existence to another. The schoolgirl took it upon herself to put around the neck of each new arrival a little collar of coloured wool so that we could tell one from another. She also had to write on the cardboard wall the name of each puppy and the time of its birth. We agreed to call the first one Malek, after a dear friend of the same name. Once the birthing process was underway the other puppies followed at fairly regular intervals. After four or five births there was a pause. We wondered if that mightn't be it. Mrs A stopped her massaging. She needed to rest. But Mélodie lifted her head, which was resting between her two front paws, and looked at the masseuse with a disconcerted expression. Her look was perfectly eloquent. Our friend from Akiruno quickly resumed her role as a midwife.

The second one was called Gatsby because the teenager was at the time reading *The Great Gatsby* with much enjoyment; the third, Jazz, the fifth, Tosca, the sixth, Amati, the seventh, Amélie, the eighth, Lulu, and, lastly, the ninth, Bartók. Mrs A continued to practise her skills in shiatsu on the belly of the birthing mother. The two hands stroked slowly in the direction of the growth of her fur. Eight little bundles of flesh of a darker or lighter sandy colour stirred as if attracted by an invisible force. When the two magical hands, pressing firmly, moved again towards the new mother's rump, she suddenly got up and gave her coach a complicit look.

'It's finished, I think.'

There was a long silence, accompanied by sighs of relief. Then some timid applause …

'*Gokurosan!* (may all your pain be blessed)', I said automatically.

I was stretched out, paralysed by pain in my lower back, not far from the space defined by the cardboard. I heard it all through the chaos of bodily sensations.

'Are you saying that to me? Or to the young mother?' asked the masseuse in an amused voice.

'To the mother of course, but to you too …'

'Is it truthful, this lie?'

TO BE SENSITIVE, TO BE COMPASSIONATE

There were peals of laughter. Barely had the start of a laugh taken hold of me than I felt a stab of pain splitting my back. I forced myself to keep my mouth shut.

But the puppies needed to be watched. Were they attaching well to their mother? Night was gradually fading. The teenage girl, who'd gone to bed long ago, had noted, in her careful handwriting, the names of the puppies until the arrival of the third, Jazz. Her mother had taken over from there.

'For the fifth one, what shall we choose?'

We didn't really know. We decided by default on whatever sounded more or less like a dog name among the music and cinema references that came to mind. Why Amati, for example? Because Mrs Suzuki, the violin teacher whom my brother had just met up with again after thirty-five years in which neither had made any contact with the other, played on a wonderful Amati. And Bartók? Julia-Madoka was working on several pieces from *Mikrokosmos*. *Amélie* obviously came from the film of that name, which she adored. Tosca from Puccini's opera, Lulu from that by Alban Berg, but also after a happy and cheerful aunt of Michèle's.

The fourth one, not named, was stillborn. Mrs A saw straight away that it wasn't alive. Hastily, she took it and wrapped it in newspaper to put it out of the mother's sight.

When the task was completed and all the little ones had begun to suckle peacefully, the mother licked them one after the other. She did the rounds of the whole litter several times, determinedly. Mrs A, exhausted after the night she'd spent tirelessly massaging the dog, finally got up and told us that she was going to take the first train home. Michèle thanked her cheerfully for her dedication and darted a furtive glance at the mother surrounded by her eight newborns. She was astounded to see her baring her fangs for a brief couple of seconds, looking up at the face of the masseuse from below. Mrs A hadn't noticed it.

Day was breaking. The intermittent sound of the newspaper deliverer's motorbike could be heard as he moved further and further away, stopping and starting. The jug boiled, the toaster's timer made a tic-tac sound as it went off. Breakfast was being prepared in the kitchen. I'd passed the rest of the night in the same place, that is to say on the floor of the living room next to the sofa. I noticed that I was covered with a big blanket that wasn't there two hours before. So I must have slept a little. I called out a pained hello to Michèle, who came over to see how I was. It was then, throwing a quick glance at the little cardboard house, that she realised that the puppies, in the absence of their mother, were snoozing on their own. 'Where is she? Where's she gone? What's happening?'

I sat down in some pain. I rested back against the sofa. Suddenly Michèle's voice came from the other end of the apartment.

'What are you doing? Aren't you looking after your little ones?'

Scarcely had Michèle's voice reached me than I saw Mélodie appear through the open glass doors of the living room. She was holding in her mouth a little toy made of yellow rubber in the shape of a crocodile. She came towards me, making little moans. She lifted her right front paw to give it to me. 'So, what have you got there, my little one?' I asked her. She let go of the toy while looking me straight in the eye.

Then she began to lick my face as if she were telling me something, as if she wanted to wipe from my face the signs of a night of pain that had been endured.

'Thank you, thank you, my friend.'

She picked up her crocodile again and went slowly towards the cardboard house. She stepped over the little low wall of about thirty centimetres we'd made as an entrance for her. She lay down near her offspring and gently placed the yellow plaything among them. Finally she put her muzzle between her dazzling white front paws and gave a deep sigh.

From that day, until the departure of the puppies and the complete demolition of the cardboard house, the yellow crocodile never again left the maternal fold.

12

PITY

ONE DAY, at the end of a period of intensifying lower back pain, I was crippled by ghastly shooting pains through my loins.

I was conducting oral exams at the university. It was a Saturday afternoon. When the last candidate had left I marked his performance and jumped up from an acute pain in my lower back. Too late. In a flash I was literally floored by what seemed like an electric shock of maximum voltage. I was lying on my back, as if paralysed. What to do? First I had to get back to my office and call my wife or an ambulance. I gathered all my remaining strength in order to get up. To start with I couldn't even turn over. Finally, with the help of a chair on which I'd sat during the orals, I managed to stand up ... I don't know how long I took to perform this simplest of movements that normally only takes a fraction of a second. Drops of sweat beaded on my brow. A sensitive ear would have picked up the sound of my teeth chattering in pain. I started to walk ... But I wasn't able to ... Still I walked ... I walked ... or, rather, I attempted something resembling human steps. I leaned against the wall of the dark corridor to put my legs one in front of the other. I sensed their proud and painful presence so strongly that it was as if they no longer belonged to me. After thirty never-ending minutes, experiencing a level of torture like nothing I'd ever known in my life, I nonetheless reached my office and succeeded in opening the door. With my left hand I reached for the telephone ... Suddenly a kind of black curtain dropped in front of my eyes.

An MRI scan revealed a severely herniated disc. After a large anaesthetic injection, which only gave me a few hours' relief, the doctor explained that I would need the patience of a player of Go and that I'd have to wait until the gelatinous core of the intervertebral disc was back in place and no longer pressed on the roots of the sciatic nerve. There was only one thing to do: stay in bed and not move. I left the hospital. It was the first time that I'd walked with a stick. An old lady stood up for me on the bus. I accepted without shame and sat down.

I returned home a little before midday. I took the prescribed analgesic medications, but they didn't take effect for some time. The pain put a complete stop to anything I felt like doing. Sitting on a chair I hated the chair; lying on my back or my side I loathed the mattress and the tatamis. Whatever position I found for myself, the aching discomfort pursued me, assailing and tormenting me without respite.

Indescribable radiating pains made me writhe in my bed. I no longer knew where to put my feet. Then I heard the sharp little sound made by Mélodie's claws when she walked on the wooden floor. The distinctive click-clack came nearer. Then, suddenly, I heard nothing more. I was lost in the dormant rage of my bruised nerves …

… I was slowly coming out of a state of blessed torpor when she gave a deep sigh. I felt her warm breath. She had lain down beside me; she had rested her muzzle on the edge of the mattress that was placed level with the tatamis. Clearly, she was waiting until I woke up. I was in darkness. I switched on my bedside lamp. It was almost seven o'clock. The happiness of having forgotten the existence of my own body was already behind me. I patted her head.

'Thank you, Mélodie, thank you.'

You could see how pregnant she was. A week later, when I was still not recovered, she would bring into the world a litter of puppies brimming with vitality.

I got up and started to walk painfully in the direction of the kitchen from which came the sound of the meal being prepared. She got up in turn and followed me.

Michèle told me that Mélodie had passed the whole afternoon next to my sick and suffering body, motionless, like a stone statue guarding the entrance to a temple. During dinner, interrupted several times by sharp pains that made me feel quite crazed and forced me to sprawl over or try desperately to find a position that, if not soothing, at least didn't produce this stabbing sensation, she remained right next to my chair, being careful not to touch my feet, which didn't really know whether they wanted to be placed on the wooden floor or to remain dangling in the air. Every time I left the table to stretch out on my back or stomach, those big round black eyes of hers stared at me from a sideways angle, without her head moving even the slightest. Then she stood up at once, her ears pricked, when I let a cry of pain escape from my mouth.

I stayed prostrate for more than two weeks, wracked with pain. I only got up to eat and to go to the bathroom. I couldn't do anything else. I did read in bed to stop myself from getting bored when I was in a little less pain thanks to the medication, but I found the continual inactivity difficult to bear. What diverted me and even succeeded in lifting my spirits a little was Mélodie's constant presence and empathetic gaze: she was there at my side night and day except at the time of her two daily walks, which Michèle and Julia-Madoka took on throughout this period. While it was still daylight she remained lying at the foot of the big marital bed, staring at the sick man each time he stirred or muttered a few ill-tempered, incomprehensible words. When night came she placed herself just next to me, the position she only took up again on the last two nights of her existence.

I wasn't going to die. But I was suffering dreadfully. Mélodie, her whole being having now become a sympathetic ear, heard the tears and my body crying out in pain. So much so that sometimes, in the middle of the night, she would make dreadful cries as if she too were being subjected to this torture.

'Don't worry, Mélodie.' Michèle's sleepy but crystal-clear voice quietly penetrated the deepening night.

Diary Extract 3

Fragments that Have Slipped from the Notebook of a Dog's Companion

It is well known that for Descartes animals were nothing more than automatons, mere machines. The Cartesian *I think, therefore I am* brings about a real rupture by distinguishing man from the other living things. Endowed with reason, thought and speech, man uproots himself from the world of living things and indeed from the world itself to take possession of it, to appropriate the position of master and possessor of the whole of nature. In a famous passage from the fifth part of the *Discourse on Method*, Descartes writes:

> If there were machines of such a kind that had the organs and aspect of a monkey, or of some other animal lacking reason, we would have no way of knowing that they were not in all respects of the same nature as these animals; whereas, if there were machines that resembled our bodies and mimicked our actions morally as much as it were possible, we would always have two very sure means of recognising that they were not on that account true men.

The first means of making this distinction is language, the second, the activity of thinking.

Malebranche, heir to the Cartesian theory of animal-machines, goes so far as to declare more clearly still: 'Thus, in animals, there is neither intelligence, nor soul as we understand it ordinarily. They eat without pleasure, they cry without pain, they grow without being aware of it, they desire nothing, they fear nothing, they know nothing...' Hence a well-known anecdote according to which Malebranche, after kicking a pregnant dog barking at a visitor, had said, 'It cries, but it has no feeling'. If an animal moans it would therefore not be an expression of pain. It would be a noise similar to the squeaking of a badly oiled or broken piece of machinery.

So it is no surprise that this insensitivity to animal suffering can extend, as Élisabeth de Fontenay points out, to a cruelty beyond telling like that shown by Father Tolbiac, admittedly a fictional character, in Guy de Maupassant's *A Life,* who, 'seeing a bitch whelp in front of some awe-struck children, disembowels her with a kick, then savagely grinds underfoot the puppies only just born and those about to be born'.

Three years before the death of Malebranche, in 1715, Rousseau was born. In 1755 he writes:

> ... as long as [man] makes no resistance to the inner compulsion to compassion he will never do harm to another man or even to any sentient being ... By these means the old arguments about the participation of animals in the law of nature can be terminated ... being related in some respects to our nature through the sensitivity with which [they] are endowed, it will be thought that they must also participate in natural law, and that man is liable to some kind of obligation towards them. Indeed, it seems that if

DIARY EXTRACT 3

> I am obliged to do no harm to my fellow, it is less because he is a reasonable being than because he is a sentient being, a quality which, being common to man and beast, must at least give to one of them the right not to be needlessly mistreated by the other.

I am obviously not a Cartesian or a follower of Malebranche. I cannot be, having spent twelve years of my life with a dog that I loved. No, when it comes down to it I'm a follower of Rousseau. The continuity between humanity and animality that was ruptured with incredible violence by Descartes and Malebranche seems in a certain way to be reinstated by Rousseau. This feeling is confirmed, in the *Discourse on Inequality*, if one reads the passage that the citizen of Geneva devotes to the notion of pity as a principle anterior to reason in the same way as love of self. He draws attention to 'the repugnance of horses to trample a living creature underfoot'. He emphasises that 'an animal does not without anxiety pass near to a dead animal of its species and that there are even some who give them a kind of burial'. But, quite clearly, mankind has followed the path of Descartes and not that of Rousseau. It has thereby arrived at almighty technoscience. We live in the age of the industrialisation of animal breeding, and of what is called zootechnics, the science of the exploitation of animal-machines. We can see the infinite distance that separates our present-day sensibility from that of Rousseau when we read the following lines taken from Book II of *Emile*:

> Pitiful man! You begin by killing the animal, and then you eat it, as if to make it die twice over. That is not enough: the dead flesh still revolts you, your entrails cannot bear it; it has to be transformed by fire, boiled, roasted, seasoned with concoctions which disguise it: you need butchers, cooks, meat roasters, people to take from

TO BE SENSITIVE, TO BE COMPASSIONATE

you the horror of the murder and dress dead bodies for you, so that the sense of taste, deceived by these disguises, does not reject what is foreign to it, and savours with pleasure carcasses whose aspect the eye itself would have found it difficult to bear.

Part II

ABSOLUTE FIDELITY: TO WAIT TILL IT KILLS YOU

13

HELP!

THE AUDIENCE WAS plunged into the ink-black darkness of the hall, separated by a big empty pit from the stage, which was lit by a bright light shining down from the black ceiling whose height I could only guess at. I was on stage, in ceremonial dress. Two violinists and a cellist were at my side. The concert was going to begin at any moment. As surprising and absurd as it seemed, I was part of a string quartet, which was going to perform one of the six masterpieces by Mozart dedicated to Haydn. I didn't recognise the musicians. My anxiety increased. Why was I there? How had I been able to accept an idea as crazy, as deluded, as that of *playing* the viola myself? In front of an audience! Here, in a place that had all the appearance of a real concert hall! What was I to do? Should I stand up and shout out that there'd been a mistake? 'Excuse me, I'm not a musician. I can't do anything … I don't know why I was brought here, why I was given this instrument that doesn't belong to me, and this black costume, which I've never worn.' I felt hot flushes spreading over my face and the whole of my body, front and back, was bathed in a cold sweat ...

A violent episode of apnoea shook me and dragged me from sleep. How long had I stopped breathing for? I was breathless, I needed air as if I'd almost drowned ... I turned to lie on my left side in order to breathe deeply.

I fell back asleep ...

It was then that I thought I heard, from beyond this night punctuated by tormenting dreams, a kind of wolf's howling, which seemed to come straight out of a fantastic story unfolding from beginning to end in a far-off Gothic kingdom that had fallen into decay.

I burrowed under the eiderdown as if to flee from the fear, to protect myself from the exhausting, nightmarish night. Yet the wolf's howls continued to make themselves heard, muffled though, their sharp, piercing notes smothered.

I emerged abruptly from my half-sleep state. I got out of bed. I was now quite sure where the piercing cries were coming from. I quickly put on my *wata-ire* (a quilted garment worn inside) and rushed to the living room: it was Mélodie who was howling in the semi-darkness, like a she-wolf howling at the full moon. Her whole body was like a trumpet which the musician points and raises high into the sky.

She'd come out of the cardboard house. I turned on the light furthest from the peacefully sleeping little puppies. She jumped up on me and, excited and quivering all over, energetically licked my hands, which were holding her two front paws. But she quickly and nimbly disengaged from our embrace to go over to one of her babies who was lost amid the chairs and magazines piled on the floor, in the shade of a big pot in which stands a ficus that is about twenty years old.

'So, it was me you were calling out to? You were howling like that to get me to help. It was an SOS! Oh, I'm sorry. I'm useless … I'm really not up to this!'

Delicately, I picked up the little one and took it back to the house, placing it among its brothers and sisters, who didn't stir at all despite this slight, unprecedented ruckus. The mother took no exception. She followed me with her eyes, attentive and benevolent. When everything was back as it should be she looked at me for a long time, her head raised. Then, a little hesitantly, she held out to me her right front paw. I crouched down to her level, face to face. I grasped her tenderly extended paw. She licked my face; then she went towards the entrance to the cardboard house. She turned around once before climbing over the little wall. At last she carefully lay down among the puppies. I said to her, 'I'm going back to bed. See you soon, Mélodie.' Her big black eyes, quite round and always a little moist, crinkled shut just as I said this, as if to give me her assent. She was soothed, reassured, calm, so calm in fact that she gave the impression she was greeting the light of dawn, which was filtering in through the fanlight.

It was from this event that seemed to date a certain intensification of the bond of affection by which the two beings, the two animals, one human, the other non-human, were already quite singularly attached to each other.

Having returned to bed I didn't go back to sleep. Again I saw the female dog-wolf howling desperately, the young mother, inexperienced and distraught, who dared not snatch

ABSOLUTE FIDELITY: TO WAIT TILL IT KILLS YOU

up her lost little deserter to return it to the space of maternal protection. Again I saw all the nerves of her slender body, which she held against me, taut, to shackle me in the close embrace of her two front legs. Again I saw her white paw hovering in the air in search of a sympathetic hand. Again I saw all the confusion and distress she showed faced with her own powerlessness in a situation beyond her control. Again, finally, I saw utter serenity returning to the mother, who, by casting her conspiratorial gaze upon me, would recover her offspring. Plaintive cries, howling jaw, unhealthily panting breath, eyes winking and blinking, ears suddenly pricking up, tail lowered and fearfully tucked between the two back legs, a distinctly perceptible quivering of the whole body: all of these in fact constituted so many signs she made for my benefit with the firm intention of engaging me, reaching me, touching me. Something, I knew, had passed between us when, in the first light of day, on moving away, I caught sight of her body stretched out in a state of complete relaxation and carefree surrender, together with *all* of her puppies, now reunited.

When they left the house a few weeks later to live their life beneath other skies, a new era began for both of us: she wanted to be right next to me as often as she could, as long as there was no one in the family who was suffering physically or mentally. Often she would even end up clinging to my legs or my arms, pressing firmly against me as if she found it unbearable for there to be a gap of a fraction of an inch between our bodies. Her shadow merged with mine. The warmth of her belly warmed my perpetually cold feet. Her deep sighs reverberated in my ears. Her warm breath suffused my lungs. Her regular breathing kept time with my heartbeat. We had become inseparable, close, very close, closer than close, to each other.

14

VOMITING

MÉLODIE HAD A number of places of her own in the apartment. In the dining room, right next to the big oval table, she had her bed where she could go to at any time to sleep, to listen to us talking at the table or to have the fur on her paws, her claws and her dew-claws cut. When Michèle said 'Come on, we're going to the hairdresser!' she went, quite naturally, although anxious and trembling a little, and placed herself on her futon, which was stuffed with little bits of wood that smelt good. It was really her home base. When our conversations became animated, heated, fired up even, she liked to move closer to us, to settle herself under the table in order to hear us better. When we relaxed in the living room she always took up a position at my feet, as if this extremity of my body were the sole lifebuoy available to her in case of an emergency or a sort of transmitter for all my sympathetic energy. At night, as I've said, she camped in our bedroom, on

VOMITING

a big mauve towel at the foot of the bed. If she wasn't asleep she pressed against the edge of our futon, which was covered in shiny, wavy hair; if she was asleep, fully stretched out, her backbone would be touching it as if she wanted to feel our presence through the warmth radiating from the marital bed. During the day, however, she mostly lay with her back against the wall, at the entrance to my study, which is also the entrance to our bedroom. That way she could see me in profile reading or typing on my keyboard.

One day, however, she found herself another, unexpected, spot. I was working at my computer. There is really no separation between my study and my bedroom. From the slightly angled ceiling that follows the slant of the roof, there falls a long *noren,* a kind of curtain, a dark navy blue, two and a half metres wide, on which are painted brightly coloured tools and utensils from Japanese popular culture of the Edo period. Sharp little moans interspersed with hiccoughs could be heard; she was dreaming. A few seconds later she woke up, got straight to her feet and then sighed deeply. She had settled herself not at the entrance to my study on my left as she usually did, but where she spent the night: that is, on the big mauve towel, behind me. I swung around on my chair.

'What were you dreaming about, my friend?'

She had her ears turned out and folded back. She took a few steps towards me and sat on her haunches, staring at me with her big round eyes filled with gentleness.

'It's a bit early for the walk. Will you let me keep working a bit longer?'

I was about to go back to my keyboard when Mélodie, hesitant, lifted her front paw, holding it out to me. I took it in my hands and thanked her warmly for this affectionate gesture. When I began to concentrate again on the screen of my computer she placed herself there on my right and this time put the other paw on my lap. I patted her head without looking at her, absent-mindedly engaging in the semblance of a one-sided conversation with her. It was at that precise moment that she exhibited an unaccustomed, strange, even disturbing form of behaviour. My desk is a large piece of wood fixed to the wall with brackets, under which are stacked shelves holding big books like the volumes of *Treasures of the French Language* and the *Grand Robert*, which means that the space between my legs and the large tomes is extremely limited and tight. But it was into that cramped little spot, naturally very uncomfortable, that my friend wanted to insinuate herself. She lay down first of all, but got up again immediately and stood up straight as a rod on her two hind legs and stared at me …

'What are you doing, Mélodie?'

She repeated the same gesture: she again gave me her right front paw, imperceptibly tilting her head to the left. I couldn't understand this unusual insistence on her part. To tell the truth, I wasn't really making any effort to listen out for the signals she was sending me so insistently. Oh, my friend! I can imagine your dismay. You could see that I wasn't reacting. We were so close to each other, we could hear each other's breathing. There was nothing between us, no more than a few centimetres. But the suffering you felt was unbearable: a solitude inflicted on you, an enforced abandonment, an imposed state of desertion … for which I can't forgive myself.

VOMITING

Distraught, she lay down again … Then, a few seconds later, she got up and came out of her cubbyhole. Advancing with little steps towards the middle of the room, she bent down and, suddenly, lowered her head towards the floor while her whole stomach began to inflate and deflate at a rapid rate like a pair of bellows being used to rekindle a fire. I understood too late the discomfort she'd expressed for my benefit, standing in front of me, with all the means she had at her disposal. I couldn't do anything other than stroke her painfully undulating stomach with the ten fingers of my two hands. Later, I saw this scene again in dreams a number of times, and I remember having had, in one dream, the disturbing vision of my arms bereft of hands and, in another, even more worrying, of my arms extending into a multitude of hands made of soft plastic that I didn't know how to use.

Finally, with a dull and painfully suffocated cry, which came up from the cavernous depths of her entrails through an involuntary retching, there suddenly spilled out a kind of dark brown gruel, in considerable quantity.

It often happens that a dog will regurgitate what is in its stomach. That's what I learned from the three or four books on canine education that my daughter had read and that I'd looked at myself when I needed to. Mélodie had had this unpleasant experience a couple of times, but without all these persistent, and vain, attempts at communication. What I found disconcerting and at the same time reassuring on each of these occasions was that she ate up again what she'd regurgitated quite happily: it was proof that it was a passing and purely functional disturbance. But that day was not the same as any of these other occasions: she didn't leap upon the soft, warm food that had just been discharged in front of her. On the contrary, she determinedly backed away a little, throwing me a look that expressed anxiety and helplessness.

I went into the kitchen to get what I needed to tackle the cleaning job like a professional. When I came back she had lain down, her muzzle placed on her front paws on the big mauve towel as if nothing out of the ordinary had happened. I wiped up the gruel and wrapped it in several sheets of advertising liftouts, which I put away in a garbage bag. I scrubbed the wooden floor vigorously with a towel soaked in detergent. Meanwhile, Mélodie got up and went out of my study, heading nonchalantly for the living room. Now that I'd got rid of the thick porridgey substance, I was trying to quench the warm and overpowering smell with a good dose of coconut detergent. Then I heard Mélodie coming back to me—she was trotting. A kind of continuous squeaking accompanied the sharp little sound that her claws made on the floor. She appeared at last and placed herself in front of me; in her mouth was the little yellow crocodile, squeaking all the while.

While she waved her right front paw in the air as if she were trying to get my attention, she made the little toy go on squeaking with no let-up. I caught hold of the extended paw and said to her, 'You're feeling better now! You're happy!'

She withdrew her right paw and gave me the other one. Then she went and settled herself on the mauve towel. She delicately released the rubber animal and placed it right next to her stomach with its shining silver fur.

'Oh yes, so that's what it was!'

At the tip of a pink teat, right beside her baby, sparkled a little pearl, snow white and lustrous.

Diary Extract 4

Fragments that Have Slipped from the Notebook of a Dog's Companion

I don't know if you can talk about friendship between a dog and its master. But I perceived in Mélodie's eyes, when she held out her paws to me one after the other to tell me that she wasn't well, something like friendship, in any case a feeling inspired by a sense of complete trust. In the moments of intense outpouring of emotion, when she clung to me as if she couldn't bear there to be so much as a hair's breadth between our bodies, I felt an indestructible bond of attachment between us. Descartes and Malebranche would have taken me for an untutored and happy fool. Rousseau would doubtless have understood me. But the one who would have agreed with me completely is Montaigne.

The age of classicism, with Descartes, saw the advent of a 'metaphysical and technical humanism' that made man a domineering sovereign exercising his power over the physical world as it was laid out before him. As for Rousseau, as I've said, he rejected the Cartesian doctrine of the animal-machine, but he appears at the same time as

ABSOLUTE FIDELITY: TO WAIT TILL IT KILLS YOU

one of the founders of modern humanism in that he emphasises the fundamental superiority of man as a free agent capable of extracting himself from the determinism of the natural world, while animals are condemned to submit to the rules imposed by nature. Perfectible (this is one of the key words of the *Second Discourse*), man becomes the agent of his own history individually as well as collectively, whereas animals do no more than repeat the same behaviours and thereby are unaware of progress, for good or ill.

Montaigne invites us into another world of thought and sensibility. With Montaigne, we are gently soothed by a feeling of reconciliation between mankind and animals. Mankind has not yet been torn from the community of living things. Chapter XII of the second book of the *Essays*, 'Apology for Raymond Sebond', teems with examples, each one as extraordinary as the next and often taken from ancient authors like Plutarch. This is one that I especially like because behind the image of the two dogs—that of King Lysimachus and that of 'one named Pyrrhus'—I see that of Mélodie, so friendly and faithful and full of gratitude ...

> As for friendship they (the beasts) have it, without comparison, more vital and more constant than men do. Hyrcanus, the dog of King Lysimachus, his master dead, remained obstinately on his bed refusing to eat or drink; and, the day that they burned his body, he ran and jumped into the fire, where he was burned. As too did the dog of one named Pyrrhus, as he did not move from the bed of his master after he died, and when he was taken away, he let himself be removed as well, and finally threw himself on to the pyre on which his master's body was burning. There are certain inclinations of affection that sometimes arise in us without the

DIARY EXTRACT 4

counsel of reason, which come from a chance temerity that others call sympathy: like us the beasts are capable of it.

To read Montaigne, even though it requires some effort to tackle his writing because of its language, which predates the radical break brought about by the rationality of classicism, is like finding a magical balm that soothes the numberless ills inflicted on the animals that are forgotten, left, neglected, abandoned, eliminated, killed, slaughtered massively and industrially, here, there and everywhere, the world over. The French language, which I have embraced and made my own over a long apprenticeship, has come out of the age of Descartes. In a sense it carries within it the trace of this fundamental divide from which it becomes possible to assign the non-human living things to the category of machines to exploit. It is sad to note that my habitual post-Cartesian language somewhat clouds my vision when I contemplate Montaigne's animal world: so abundant, so generous, so benevolent.

15

PUNISHMENTS

THE DAILY WALK constitutes a vital activity for a dog. It is a form of exercise, an expenditure of physical energy essential to the maintenance and continuance of a healthy life. We used to have two walks a day: in the morning before breakfast, or after, if I didn't go off to work, and in the evening, mostly after dinner.

But to go for a walk with a dog is to introduce it into the world of humans where a social civility prevails, to expose it to their sometimes pitiless stare and judgement. It was therefore necessary to teach Mélodie a minimum of rules of behaviour: to walk beside her master at the pace he set, to relieve herself in the gutter, to wait for the green light before crossing the street, not to bark needlessly when she met another dog ... As amazing, as incredible as it seems, she didn't need repeated training to internalise the rules and prohibitions. I don't remember there being difficult or painful moments in socialising her. The pedagogical satisfaction of this teacher was greater with her than it was with some frankly lazy students who lacked the desire to progress. Twice, however, only twice, did I scold her and hit her mercilessly; I had to force myself to harden my heart, make it impervious to any cry of despair, with a devil's heart.

The first time was right at the beginning. The protection offered by the vaccine had not yet taken effect and she was not able to go out and play in the street. With the stress of this mounting, every day at nightfall, as I've already mentioned, she would suddenly be overcome by the desire to run frantically through the apartment; she would bark her head off, but I was unable to attribute any meaning to the explosion of yelps. The obsessive running around the house would cease, I thought, once we took her out regularly morning and evening. As for her habit of continual yelping, we had to act quickly to nip it in the bud. If not, we imagined that neighbourly good relations would suffer. So I hit the poor creature a number of times on her rump with a sixty-centimetre bamboo ruler that had belonged to my 88-year-old mother and was now part of the sewing kit of my French wife. No doubt Mélodie was astounded to see the mood of her always kindly master suddenly transformed into this incomprehensible satanic rage. But the cruelty of the master's heart of stone made him twist the knife in the wound. He took the dog's tail and lifted up the weight of ten or so kilos, shaking it and inflicting resounding whacks with the ruler as he did so.

After that day the disruptive yelping stopped altogether. The animal never barked again unless she had to tell us something, to deliver an urgent message to us.

The second occasion involving punishment came about in Philosophy Park, which was, in effect, the meeting place for the dogs of our district. Towards six o'clock in the evening, winter and summer, at a time when the passers-by were thinning out, from around and about there came to play a number of dogs of different sizes and ages who had got to know each other. Among them there was a young Labrador called Tom who was an indefatigable chaser of balls. His master would throw the ball as far into the distance as he could and Tom, never tiring, would retrieve it. As for Mélodie, this game, so universal and typically canine had never interested her. But, that day, impressed perhaps by Tom's ardour, she clearly wanted to have fun with her companion's round yellow plaything. The two masters agreed to get them to compete against each other. Tom's master threw the ball a few times in a row. The two animals charged off at once as if the little spherical object, transformed into a magical whirlwind, was drawing them up with extraordinary power. Tom, who read the slightest movement made by his master and therefore guessed the direction of the flying object in a split second, succeeded in catching it before his newly arrived competitor. Tom's master suggested that I now have a turn at throwing the tennis ball. I accepted. But it made no difference; Tom was more skilful and better trained for the task than my dog. It seemed to me that Mélodie ran faster than her rival, but she didn't manage to get herself into the best position in relation to the ball to snatch it up deftly.

Even so, after several attempts, she finally succeeded in grabbing hold of it by fending off the advances of her male adversary, while the latter, disappointed by his failure, became angry and wanted to get possession of the coveted object. The winner would not back down. As a result the scene suddenly turned to one of hostility, which neither I nor Tom's master was expecting. The female dog yelped violently, showing her fangs. Tom did the same. And the two animals began to fight unrestrainedly. I was gripped by a growing sense of terror. Without giving it any thought, I was impelled to intervene in this brawl, which had every chance or mischance of degenerating on both sides into a sad and costly visit to the vet. I forcefully separated my dog from Tom, whipping her with all my strength with the rope leash the colour of blood. Tom, perhaps frightened by my sudden appearance, had taken off like a little rascal. His master was trying to catch him but he had given him the slip and was now running around the water point. As for the conqueror of the yellow ball, her whole body was trembling before her kind protector who had suddenly turned into a cruel and implacable overlord. He didn't weaken, however. The stinging lashes with the leash continued. He didn't let up. He only stopped when she'd abandoned her booty. Piercing cries of pain could be heard. Beneath the assumed mask of a twisted tyrant, Mélodie's master hated himself and wept. He begged a thousand pardons of his non-human friend for whipping and torturing her like that.

Finally the ball fell and rolled to the ground.

The instrument of torture was abandoned.

I crouched down and removed my mask. I brought my face close to hers, stroking it over and over again, arrested in this attitude of reconciliation. Palpating her as if I were a master magician, I kept repeating the words '*gomen ne, gomen ne, gomen ne* … (forgive me, forgive me, forgive me …)', infantile words which sounded like the refrain of a prayer. Like an open wound, the feeling of the red leash, suddenly transformed into a whip, and striking Mélodie's back, has stayed with me, a scar that has never healed.

16

WALKS

MÉLODIE HAD INTERNALISED the rules of behaviour through the education I'd given her, the only possible way for the canine species to live in harmony with humans. It's not part of my thinking that dogs must be left to go free ... Natural and absolute freedom for animals, as for humans, would lead to the law of the strongest, to anarchy, to a state of permanent war, latent or real: in short, to the very impossibility of life. The theory and the fiction of the social pact as Rousseau conceives of and elaborates them start from an acknowledgement of this fact.

Men are free and equal in the state of nature. They enjoy natural and absolute freedom, natural law if one prefers, because there is no power that transcends them, that is placed above them. However, in this state, sooner or later, 'the obstacles that are harmful to their preservation' finish by overcoming 'the forces that each individual can employ' to remain in it. So, says Rousseau, 'this primitive state can no longer persist, and the human species would perish if it did not change its way of being'. The state of nature, the reign of natural law, is fragile in itself and necessarily ends in a generalised fratricidal war. Hence the necessity of adopting another way of living, radically different, through this artefact that is the social pact. The state of nature is a state without law, or rather a state in which natural law only prevails as a potentiality because of the absence of any public force outside of individuals capable of giving it effect. Society, constructed by men brought together by means of a social contract, sets out to actualise natural law or, in other words, to produce a common space in which men find their liberty at the higher level of civil life.

The freedom regained in civil life resides, then, in learning the limits imposed on each individual, since it is this individual training that is the very basis of the coexistence of multiple freedoms. Hence the fundamental role of education, which is, according to Henri Peña-Ruiz, a 'process by which a being is led along, conducted (from the Latin *ducere*) towards a pre-determined point, starting from an initial condition from which it is necessary to emerge (*ex-ducere*).'

The education that I gave Mélodie had no purpose other than that of allowing her to enjoy the greatest freedom in the life that was hers, as seen from the perspective of her relationships with me, with my family and with the human society around her. Giving her strict rules was the only way to make her free.

WALKS

The morning walk was a true moment of happiness for me. I would like to think that it was the same for her. It was the time I could take pleasure in walking with her as my companion, feel the delight of a season in the subtle variations of temperature as well as in the light perfume carried on the breeze, stop and admire what was there to be admired: the cherry trees in flower in springtime, the maple leaves turning red in autumn, in winter the distinct outline of Fuji-san in the distance against the remarkably limpid sky. As for her, she busied herself intently with making a reading, a decoding, of the world by sensory means whose intricacies I was clearly unable to imagine. Often off the leash, she was perfectly aware of when, or in what situation, she could take the liberty of going away from her master, letting herself be led by her sense of smell. She would come back when I called her. She stopped and sat on her behind when I waited for the green light to cross the street. At the approach of a small specimen of her own kind that, on seeing her, began to emit a series of shrill little yaps, she showed an impassive serenity, supremely imperturbable in her composure.

The morning walks were sometimes reduced to the shortest distance for purely human, work-related reasons. Even so, the morning walk was generally longer than the evening one. The strolls tended to lengthen noticeably when it was fine and, especially, when I was accompanied by Michèle and/or Julia-Madoka.

One winter Sunday, in a glorious excess of luminosity—the light having the brightness of jewels glinting in the sun as often happens in Tokyo in winter—I left early in the morning with Mélodie to follow a route of middling length.

ABSOLUTE FIDELITY: TO WAIT TILL IT KILLS YOU

We were planning to make a family visit to my mother's, and the walk had therefore to be cut short. On leaving the house we made our way as usual towards Nakano Avenue, a big boulevard in our neighbourhood. Needing to relieve herself, she went into a corner partly hidden by azaleas. I had a canvas bag containing a big bottle of water and a dozen advertising liftouts from the morning's paper. I took out the bottle and poured out half of it to wash away the yellow liquid. After some dozens of yards she stopped to relieve herself again. I put an advertisement for Uniqlo between her two back legs. No longer constrained, she sat down next to me, giving me time to pick up her faeces and wrap them carefully in two or three sheets of glossy paper. 'Come on! Let's go!'

We set off on our route. First we took the little street that rises to lead into the street on which the Araiyakushi station is situated. Coming to the little intersection from which three laneways branch off, we took the narrowest of the three, barely two metres wide. We followed the path edged by little wooden houses with tiny gardens crammed with little pots of bonsai. On the Katayama footbridge, which straddles Nakano Avenue, she stopped to sniff the overhanging branches of the cherry trees. They already had some buds. We continued, passing beneath the huge walnut tree planted in the raised garden of Mr M's house. At the end of the lane we took the street that connects Nakano Avenue and the Miyoshoji Canal at right angles, a street that was much wider but as quiet as the laneway we'd just left. Having passed in front of the very old house in the style of a bygone era that belonged to Mrs K, and that faces a big, modern, upmarket building of three levels, we finally arrived at the canal. I chose to walk along it instead of following the path by the Hyakkannon memorial garden of Numabukuro, which would have made the walk too long. We had to get home quite quickly in order to be able to leave before nine o'clock to take advantage of the uncongested Sunday traffic. The path by the canal with its hedge of assorted bushes had no patches of shade. We headed into the sun; I was dazzled, in fact blinded, by the ricochets of silver light. A couple of dog walkers were coming along on the other side of the street, but I could barely make them out through my half-closed eyes. Leaving the canal behind us, we made our way along a street in the shade of the houses and buildings. We returned at last to our starting point. A red light prevented us from crossing Nakano Avenue. Not a car in sight. But I waited for the light to turn green, standing beside my companion, who did the same, immobile in her sitting position.

At home they were waiting for me to return, so that we could leave. I had to explain to Mélodie the reason for our being away for the day. She looked me in the eye, unflinching. Our things were in the hallway; under my arm I had the little bag containing my driver's licence—she was perfectly aware that we were going in the car. As I was telling her that we wouldn't be away for very long and that we'd try to get back in the afternoon before sunset, she jumped up on me, standing on her back legs for as long as she could manage, pinioning me with all her strength. I let Michèle and Julia-Madoka leave, and I said to her several times over, 'See you soon. There's really no need to worry, we'll be back again very quickly.' Before closing the front door completely I held it ajar for a few seconds as I tried to fathom the look she kept fixed on me. It said, 'Why are you doing this to me?'

My mother lives an hour and a half from us, at Machida, on the Odakyu train line, with my brother and his family. The lunch we shared brought together the whole household, and we spent the beginning of the afternoon together. The conversation was intense and high-spirited—it centred on the crisis of transmission, which, all over the world, afflicts schools and educational systems. But, really, I was miles away. I was thinking about the one who was waiting for us at home or, rather, waiting for me, who did nothing but wait for me. No doubt she'd be in the hall, in exactly the same spot I'd left her as we went off. She'd be lying down with her head on her front paws, dozing. Low sighs would accompany her soaring dreams, and from time to time she'd be making heart-rending moans.

I said to my mother that I wanted to go home sooner than expected. I explained why. She replied that she understood. Then she recalled a stray dog that I had picked up, one rainy day, on the way home from school.

It was raining torrents that day. In a laneway that followed the contours of a bamboo grove and led down to the street in front of our house I met a dog, like Tintin's Snowy, lost and soaked to the bone. Instead of a collar it had a long rope of rice straw tied around its neck. It was skinny. Our eyes met despite the little child's umbrella sheltering me and that no doubt hid me a little. I approached it and asked it if it was by itself, if there was no adult with it ... I headed towards the house. When I'd taken twenty steps I turned around. It was still looking at me. I took pity on it. I retraced my steps and took hold of the rope, to which it made no objection. I led it along the private walkway, next to our house, which was used by the tenants of a shack belonging to my parents. I tied the wet dog to the tree that stood right in the middle of the walkway. I told it to wait for me ... As I opened the sliding door of the back entrance (which was only for the everyday use of the family, and for permitted merchants when they called), I shouted out, '*Tadaima!* (I'm home now!)'. I didn't conceal anything from my mother. She wanted to see the dog. She opened a big black umbrella, I ducked out. The ground, not yet bitumened over (that didn't happen until the 1970s), was muddy. The heavy rain, mixing with the black mud, spattered the poor dog. It was just like in the magnificent final combat scene of *Seven Samurai*, which has always reminded me of that day of driving rain. It was there, still dripping with rain. I asked my mother for a little food for the dog, which was all alone, tired, soaking wet, hungry and thirsty ... My mother listened to me and let me have my way. She put some white rice in a big bowl and poured miso soup over it. As she held out this improvised meal she said finally, 'But you must part with it. We can't keep it. Do you understand?'

I nodded my head as I grabbed the bowl and rushed to the sad, famished creature. I crouched down in front of it and gave it the food. It emptied the big bowl and stared at me for a long time. Drops of water that kept on falling from its eyelids gave me the strange impression that it was crying in silence as it bore all the weight of the world ... My memories dry up at this point. Nothing that happened after that has stayed with me. I don't know anything of the way in which I parted from this friend of one day ... In fact, I don't even know with certainty if, more than fifty years ago, the child that I was really lived the scene in the way that I've just described it ... What is absolutely certain, though, is that I told myself this story more than once, many years later, in an act of memory and remembrance and that I shared it with my mother, who didn't forget it. The real is out of reach. It is the recollection, perpetually renewed and refreshed, that replaces the real in merging with it.

I took the wheel, and immediately turned into the still freely flowing motorway. We reached home before night fell. I climbed the stairs four at a time. As I turned the key in the lock I could see, through the front door's little pane of reinforced glass, Mélodie's tail, wagging furiously. I crossed the threshold and went into the apartment. She stood up on her back legs and took me between her front ones just as she'd done when I left. I squatted down to make her feel at ease. She rolled onto her back, her vulnerable belly displayed without care or fear, and I stroked it gently all along its length. The joy at regaining her master got the better of her self-control; all the tensed muscles let go at once: she could no longer stop herself from urinating. Amazed or embarrassed by this moment of incontinence, she got up again quickly and moved a few steps away. I was struck by the reddish appearance, a little like rosé wine, of the little puddle of water. 'That's blood', I said to myself. The women came over to me. I was worried and I said, 'She couldn't hold on, she was so happy. But there's blood in her pee.'

'Is it serious?' asked the teenage girl.

'No, I don't think so', said her mother. 'But we'll have to phone Mr D to see what he thinks.'

So I telephoned Mr D, the vet who knew her from the first vaccinations. I gave him all the information about the situation. He told me that it was probably because of the stress of the painful separation of half a day that we'd put her through.

I clasped Mélodie in my arms and said to her in a deliberately upbeat tone, 'We'll go for a walk while it's still daylight!'

She reacted immediately by jumping up. Then she positioned herself at the entrance, ready to leap forward as soon as the door opened. She saw that the whole family was getting ready. We heard then for the first time little repeated moans of impatience that sounded like a baby's babbling.

No wind. Mild temperature. The fine weather was continuing. The four of us departed in the fading, fleeting light of dusk. She walked briskly on my left, off the leash. We went the same way as we had that morning. From time to time she allowed herself to get a few yards ahead, but it was to stop at a particular spot to tell us that it was just there that she wanted to stop. Again she sniffed the branches of the cherry trees in bud on the Katayama Bridge. Thanks to her and this stop that she insisted on making, we became aware of the subtle arrival of spring, as the fragrance that heralds its arrival was not yet really perceptible. When she reached the canal, where the path divides, she repeated the same gesture: this time she went further ahead, ten metres or so, and watched us catching up to her, keeping quite still and attentive. Day gave way to night. The straight pathway by the canal was now lit by street lamps spaced at regular intervals of about thirty metres.

'We'll go along by the canal, if that's OK with you', I said to my walking companions.

'Yes, let's head home. I have to get on with the cooking …'

We had started making our way along the canal walkway and had already gone about ten metres when I turned around to check if Mélodie was following us. But she wasn't. She was still in the same place, still not moving, except that now she was sitting.

'What are you doing, my friend?'

She got up again and turned her head towards the street leading to the Hyakkannon memorial garden of Numabukuro. It was obvious that she was indicating the direction she wanted to go in.

'You want to go that way! You're enjoying this walk together as a family and you want to keep it going, is that it? And quite right too!'

An angelic smile spread over the face of the teenage girl. Her mother, tenderly complicit, put up no resistance to what the young girl and her animal sister both wanted. We were amazed at this way of letting us know what she wanted, and happy, too, knowing that she felt and showed joy in this family walk at nightfall. We continued our evening stroll into an adjoining neighbourhood, namely that of Numabukuro, which is perceived as not quite ours, given that in this country the geographical imaginary is basically constructed around the closest railway or subway station.

The garden of the Hundred Statuettes of the Merciful Goddess was closed. During the day the children from the preschool next door come there to play, but once night falls no one dares to venture into this dark zone inhabited by the dead. So we made our way towards the vibrant, bustling station, which was disgorging a mass of men and women, many of whom were accompanied by children. We crossed at the level crossing. Far from being frightened by the forest of moving legs, Mélodie went along calmly beside me. Given the crowd, I'd taken the precaution of putting her on the leash, but since she was walking at the same pace as me, she almost didn't need it. Ascending the broad slope that leads to the heart of the district, we reached the entry to the Park of the Peaceful Forest. We entered the park without hesitation, as if the blue silence of the giant trees was tugging at us and pulling us in. With the earbuds of their iPods in their ears, a few joggers, running with their shadows around the dimly lit 400-metre oval track, seemed to amplify the burden of urban solitude that was their constant companion.

'It's a bit like the atmosphere of *My Neighbour Totoro*, Dad.'

'Oh, do you think so?'

'Look! Look at Fuji-san! It's so beautiful!'

The mother was an unfailing admirer of the magnificent mountain, for her the provider of invigorating energy. It excited her to see its silhouette, enlarged, quite black, which stood out against the last red rays of the setting sun. Taking her daughter with her, she went to climb the little hillock from which the sacred mountain can be seen more clearly. I followed them with Mélodie. Three human beings and one non-human stood clasped together and formed just a single shadow.

On returning to the house, Mélodie slept deeply. She didn't wake up during the night. She didn't growl; she didn't dream. The next morning her urine was copious, and it bore no traces of red.

17

THE SHOWER

MY WALK WITH Mélodie was a daily activity that I didn't allow myself to forgo, because for her it was an absolute necessity—whether it was good weather or bad, hot or cold, raining or snowing, it was my unvarying habit to get out with her at least for a short stroll. But the task of showering her arose from a different imperative, namely the human need to maintain the family space in a certain state of cleanliness.

These days, it is a fairly well-known fact that the Japanese take off their shoes in the entrance before stepping into the private interior domain of domestic space. The cleanliness of the inside, or more precisely the feeling they have about it, is affirmed not only by the way the doors and windows are so tightly sealed, but also by the more or less significant difference in level of the clean living environment in relation to the dirty ground. The ground floor of a Japanese house in its traditional conception never being at street level, there is a quite marked difference in level of twenty to thirty centimetres between the concrete floor of the entrance and the wooden floor of the hallway. In Japan, instead of entering a house you go up into it. And it's in this movement of going up that you take off your shoes. That is why shoes are not part of the clothing of the Japanese in the strict sense, because when they are in the house, the domain of cleanliness, they go about barefoot, or rather, I should say, they are scrupulous in avoiding walking with their shoes on as they are, necessarily, dirty.

As for dogs, naked from top to toe, so to speak, they have no shoes to take off. It is that, doubtless, which causes them to be thought unworthy of crossing the threshold to go up into the house and enter the space of familial intimacy. Usually they remain in their kennel, placed, as can be seen, for example, in Seijirō Kōyama's film *Hachi-ko* (1987), near the *engawa*, the open walkway that leads directly into the garden.

For us the situation was different. We didn't want Mélodie to remain alone outside, deprived of freedom of movement, whether tied up or shut in. We judged that she had the right to the inside as a fellow team member in the life we all shared. For that it was necessary that her paws were perfectly clean. So a ritual became established: instead of removing the shoes that she didn't have, we cleaned or even washed her paws in the front hall after each outing, each walk.

As it happened, though, the demand for cleanliness applied not just to her paws, as the tatamis, the cushions, the walls she leant against, in fact anything and everything that was in her path, became dirty, visibly blackened from contact with her unwashed body. Hence the idea of showering her regularly, once every three weeks.

Our bathroom, like that of any Japanese house, is a space equipped with a shower and a big bath, all set up in a room that is closed by a sliding door of frosted glass, an area of around two by one and a half metres. We get undressed in the corner next to the ablutions area, where the washbasin is and all the bath things are kept. I could have taken a bath with her as, in the past, my father or mother would take a bath with my brother and me when we were little. I used to sit submerged up to the neck in the warm water that filled the big bath. It was made of cypress and gave off a strong fragrance. And I often played with a water pistol as I talked with my father, his scarlet face perspiring with big drops of sweat as the steam wafted up to the ceiling in a shimmering mist. It's one of the oldest and happiest memories of my childhood—no hint of anxiety, no thought of the future.

Sharing the same bath water is a mark of the greatest familiarity, the greatest affection, the greatest tenderness. A scene from *There Was a Father* (1942), directed by Yasujirō Ozu, comes to mind: it is in the waters of the big bath of a country inn that the son reveals to his father his long repressed wish to live with him. More than once I'd thought of taking a bath with Mélodie, but, fearing that I'd shock my wife, I didn't dare ... However, the idea is perhaps not as ridiculous as it seems: in *Hachi-ko*, which I mentioned earlier, we see Professor Shujiro Ueno (played by Tatsuya Nakadai) and his dog Hachi-ko immersed in a warm bath, which gives them a deep sense of closeness and wellbeing.

THE SHOWER

Throughout Mélodie's life, washing and showering her was a task that always fell to me, except just once when I could not do it because of the herniated disc that had immobilised me.

When a session in the shower had been decided on, I undressed and, stark naked, went into the bathroom a few minutes before her, first to get warm and then to assemble everything that was needed for grooming her. I called Mélodie when I was ready for her. Michèle brought her to the bathroom. She came hesitantly; her head was always slightly lowered, no doubt to show that she really didn't want me to perform this systematic and methodical washing of her entire body. But she would hear my insistent call and resign herself to it in the end. Once she'd finally stepped inside the shower alcove I closed the door and began spraying her. At the beginning she stood on her four feet. But very quickly she sat down and didn't take her eyes off me, keeping them half closed. I lathered her copiously with shampoo, twice, from the neck to the tail via the stomach where her coat, milky white, was especially thick. To rinse her off I needed her to stand up again on her four legs; keeping the showerhead in my right hand, I slid my left hand under her belly. She got up again at once to make it easier for me.

A couple of times in the course of the session she would feel the need to shake herself vigorously like a dog that gets out of the water after a mad dash into a river. As a result she sprayed me liberally with the drops of water she shook off her coat. At the end of it all I was as soaked as she was, as if I'd washed myself completely at the same time. That's why I'd stopped wearing my underpants. My role was not simply that of an employee of a dog grooming business; rather, I shared, in my naked state, the same bathwater as companion or fellow partaker of the shower, if I can put it like that. Yes, I was naked, nude before the one who never stopped looking at me. I was looked at, I felt myself looked at by my dog throughout this process of common and reciprocal ablutions, particularly as, sitting on a little wooden seat that allowed me to be on the same level as she was, I was facing her and my penis was exposed to her gaze. She never looked at my genitals, but by lowering her head she could easily see them and, in any case, see them she did. But I had no sense of embarrassment at that moment, sitting there naked; I had no shame about my nudity facing an animal that wasn't nude precisely because it was nude from the very first and for always. As you might have suspected, what comes to mind for me is the incredible book by Jacques Derrida *The Animal That Therefore I Am*. At the starting point of his philosophical meditation on the question of animality/humanity, Derrida notes the critical experience of the feeling of embarrassment or modesty aroused by the fact of having been seen nude, naked, by his cat. In my case, I felt no modesty, no embarrassment in the strict sense of the term. I carried on the grooming of my dog in all tranquillity: we were situated, symmetrically, in a state of nudity that, after all, wasn't one, either for her or for me.

On the other hand, it wasn't the same thing with my wife and I when we felt the stirring of desire and wanted to make love. Each time, without fail, I was overcome by a paralysing sense of modesty. To make love in Mélodie's presence or to be seen by her making love was unthinkable. We had to ask her to go out of the bedroom if she was there. If she was somewhere else we had to shut the door, which, most of the time, was left wide open. And just the sound of the door being closed (even though it didn't make an excessive squeaking sound) aroused Mélodie's attention and prompted her to come and lie down in front of it. During our silent lovemaking, when we forgot the world, I sometimes thought that I could hear the sighs of the dog languishing on the other side of the door.

Once washed, she had to be dried with a towel. When she'd shaken herself for the last time I wrapped her in a big bath towel, which I rubbed against her skin as I used to do with my daughter when she was three or four years old. When no more drops of water fell from her coat I opened the glass door of the bathroom to let her go out. This she did without me saying anything to her. And, inevitably, she shook herself one more time with all her strength, as if the water that had penetrated down to the roots of her fur was an irritating foreign body, like a tiny grain of rice lodged between the teeth.

The bath things tidied away, I stayed under the shower for a few minutes more to get warm, except in summer. When I came into the living room, dressed or bare-chested with just a towel around my waist, I saw her lying down, relaxed, near the big table, next to the bay window, especially when it was fine in winter. I sat down in the sun as well to dry myself and dry my hair.

'Well, did that make you feel good? You smell so nice now!'

I held my hand out to her. She raised her right paw, a little clumsily. I took it. She licked my extended hand, slowly, carefully.

The next day and for several days after the shower the whole floor was strewn with golden hairs, which shone in the sun. Sometimes they clumped into balls of fluff. We would vacuum twice a day, but our socks would still be covered in this golden fur when we took them off at night before going to bed.

Now that she's no longer here the fur has completely disappeared. Immediately after Mélodie died, taking the advice of the vet who was amazed that our dog had remained beautiful up until the end, Michèle cut and knotted together two little strands of her hair as a kind of memento. At first they remained next to the candleholder, but after the cremation they were placed with her red collar, the metal part now quite rusty, on the big square box containing the urn.

One day, at the bottom of the holey pockets of the worn green Loden cape that I'd bought in Montpellier a good many years before, a coat I only wore in winter for my daily outings with Mélodie, I found a pair of navy blue woollen gloves that I thought I'd lost forever. They were very dirty and mud-stained. But what disturbed me were the coarse hairs that had collected on them and that I'd never really noticed. I removed the hairs one by one and carefully put them together. Then I made a strand of them and tied it together with a little red ribbon. I put it beside the two others.

Night was falling. I lit a little candle that shone on the large photo of Mélodie that faced her urn.

18

A STILLBIRTH

IT IS SAID that Japanese dogs—Shiba or Akita—have the characteristic of really only becoming attached to their master. Exclusive affection for one particular being signifies indifference, distrust, if not aggressiveness, towards others. I've read somewhere that the Akita, for example, might show no interest in strangers in the street or guests to the house.

This was not the case with our golden retriever. At home, with us, she was calm and serene, like an autumn sky after a typhoon, so much so that we sometimes forgot she was there. The discreet sound of her footsteps, the occasional sighs or plaintive little cries brought on by dreams and often accompanied by slight convulsive shudders of her legs reminded us of her pleasant and enlivening company. But as soon as someone rang at the door and was greeted as a faithful and trustworthy friend, she suddenly turned into a demonstrative ball of energy. Her master and his family came first in her show of affection, but her inexhaustible need to express the warmth of her feelings would, if need be, take her beyond the tight-knit family circle.

It was a summer day at the end of an afternoon that made you hope for the general cooling brought about by elderly neighbours who, wanting to carry on the tradition of old times, would copiously water the street. A midwife paid us a visit. We'd become close through a French woman who'd chosen to have a home birth, far from the heavily medicalised structures of the big hospital centres. Having agreed to run a midwives' training course in Madagascar, she had come to talk over her concerns about communication barriers with the trainees. She was accompanied by her son, who was in the midst of swotting for his exams and who, she said, loved dogs.

We went and sat in the living room. On the glass table there was an old edition of *I'm Expecting a Baby*, which had been given to us many years ago by a woman friend of ours, a psychoanalyst, when we learnt that Michèle was pregnant. Another more austerely scientific book that I'd found in a corner of my library, *Practical Manual of Sophrological Preparation for Motherhood*, was also on the table. These were all that we could lend the midwife. Michèle told her that she'd found valuable information in some of the pages of these two books, which both had a wealth of illustrations and photographs. The midwife asked her if she had any other children apart from the girl she'd seen two or three times on one of our evening walks with the dog. The hostess replied that she'd had nothing but unhappy experiences after the birth of her daughter and confided in her that if she'd known her at the time of her second and third pregnancies her family life might perhaps have been different.

A STILLBIRTH

Through the windowpanes of the door that separates the hall from the living room we could see the dog sitting on her back legs. From time to time she tapped delicately on the door. We could hear the scratching sound made by the hesitant and halting contact of her claws with the glass. The midwife suggested to Michèle that she let her come in. As soon as the door opened she charged straight in and was all over the guest who'd liberated her.

'OK, OK … Calm down … Calm down!'

The college student, who hadn't said a word up until then, took the two paws from his mother's lap, said to her that she was going about it the wrong way and explained how to pat the dog and avoid all that licking. Mélodie turned to the teenager—and began licking his face vigorously.

The unexpected meeting between the midwife and the exuberant dog who'd brought eight puppies into the world naturally led Michèle to recount the story of the stillborn puppy and the yellow crocodile that the mother adopted as a needed imaginary substitute.

'That's quite normal. The little puppy shouldn't have been hidden from her. In fact someone should have shown it to her … It's like a woman who's had a miscarriage …'

I was only half listening to the female conversation. But a little shiver ran through me when the midwife uttered the word *miscarriage*. I looked at my wife, who wasn't looking at her guest. It seemed to me that, for a moment, she was in another world.

ABSOLUTE FIDELITY: TO WAIT TILL IT KILLS YOU

It was raining that day. The huge door of the delivery room slid open slowly. A midwife in her fifties came towards me. She held something in her hands, wrapped in a pure white cloth.

'It was a boy ... You know, when it rains like it is today there are twice as many births ... But your baby came out much too soon ... unfortunately. I haven't shown him to your wife. Do you want to see him?'

'Yes.'

It was a human baby, almost completely formed, but tiny and extremely fragile, like a baby doll, about fifteen centimetres long. He seemed to be sleeping in the outstretched hand of the midwife, like a child who dreams while sleeping in the hand of a great Buddha, tenderly held open like a huge orchid. The white cloth covered the little naked body. Then he disappeared behind the big door.

Michèle stayed in hospital for several days, long enough to accompany the child back to the kingdom of souls and to return again.

Meanwhile I went to see my parents to tell them about what had happened. My father took out his calligraphy things. He began to rub the charcoal stick on the ink stone whose hollow was filled with water. When he'd prepared the Chinese ink, he wrote, with a little brush, four ideograms, which were arranged vertically:

幻
星
童
児

A STILLBIRTH

Immaculate child of a dream star. It was the name (a little Buddhist in flavour) that, as an experienced monk, he had devised for the child who had been born prematurely and was no more. The name Jean-Emmanuel that we'd thought of one day, Michèle and I, in the beguiling vision of a rose-coloured future, has remained with us forever in our memory as a couple. My father, a little flushed from a quickly swallowed cup of sake, held out to me the calligraphied sheet of paper, which, on my return, I put away at the back of one of the drawers of my desk like a hidden treasure. Then life went on again with the return of the bereft mother. Some years later, when my father had left us, I finally had the courage to show Michèle the magical, stellar name that he'd given to our stillborn baby boy. I remember the absent and distant look she gave me at the time.

I wondered if the word *miscarriage* hadn't reopened the old scar, if it didn't make the mother dream about her *immaculate child of a dream star*, the child she hadn't seen and who, all things considered, should have been shown to her lying in the compassionate hand that served as his bed ...

The dog kept up her warm welcome to the midwife and her son. It seemed she made no distinction between her master and his guests in her show of affection. This rather extraordinary ability is far from being shared by all human beings, and it was demonstrated brilliantly during an evening party that was a little special, an occasion we'd wanted our daughter to enjoy at the time when she was coming of age.

19

AN EVENING PARTY

TO CELEBRATE TURNING fifty a Parisian friend had the idea of getting some friends together in the country house he'd inherited in Normandy and that, as a Sunday handyman, he'd been enjoying spending his time patiently renovating over many months. The renovations were still far from finished, but he sent out more than a hundred invitations to friends all over the world, and about eighty people replied that they were coming. Working at the other end of the planet, all we could do was write him a long letter to congratulate him on this happy undertaking. The party, where men and women of I don't know how many different cultural backgrounds mixed together, was a wonderful occasion, my friend told me later.

His account of the party set me thinking. It didn't occur to me to do the same for my fiftieth birthday, but if I'd wanted to, how many invitations could I have sent out to different parts of the world? Of course, in my culture of origin there's definitely something false, affected or even pretentious, in the very idea of celebrating one's birthday. But leaving that aside, how many friends would I have had around me at a party I didn't for a second imagine myself having? How many people beyond the family circle could I have asked to come and share the pleasure of being together?

It is said that this country is inhabited by eight million gods. Eight million is the metaphor for the infinite or numberless, like Don Giovanni's *mille e tre* (1003: the number of his Spanish conquests). I can imagine the mental universe of the archipelago's inhabitants being turned upside down by the arrival, in the sixth century, of the universal principle that Buddhism embodied. At that time each clan, each tribe, each village, each local community had their own gods to protect them. Did they feel the need to reach out to the Other in its difference amid this motley and divided array? No, I don't think they did. You lived in keeping with the cult of your gods, and you could forget about all the rest. You were very close to your neighbours. You could almost touch them. But you didn't see them or feel them. Does this ancient and millennial epoch live in me? Does it constitute one of the deepest layers of my being? Am I determined by the sediments of this collective past? Who am I?

For Christmas, in 2003 or 2004, I had planned a gathering at our home that would bring together a dozen or so people. Given the size of our apartment this was the maximum number we could think of inviting. I set myself a challenge: that of diversity. My intention was not to compete with my Parisian friend but to follow his example in surrounding myself with a diverse mix of people. I invited some of our friends and friends of my daughter's—people of my age, young people and the not-so-young—men and women who for the most part didn't know each other. There were French people, a cultural attaché from the embassy and an unemployed PhD in sociology who was looking for a teaching position; there was a Moroccan who wasn't bound by the dietary prescriptions of his religion and his Cameroonian girlfriend, who, unlike him, was careful to adhere to them; there was a young African American, the friend of a friend, who'd come to present me with a colourful cowboy waistcoat; there was a Canadian woman of Haitian origin who wrote poems; there was a young Chinese woman, a Uighur, on a study trip to Tokyo, who did the tango and didn't eat pork; there was a French-German atheist who was culturally Jewish, and a Palestinian woman who asked to leave the gathering and go and pray in a quiet corner of the apartment; there was a German of Turkish origin who, after brilliant studies in Tokyo, had found a job in a Japanese firm. And finally, amid this whole mixture of cultures, religions and dietary habits, there was us and a Japanese couple, a very old friend who'd worked in finance for a long time and who, with his wife, was now enjoying the peaceful life of a retiree ... What made it possible to gather together so many different individuals to make up this engaging company for an evening was the fact that there was one language that they all shared. They all spoke French. They spoke it more or less well, but they spoke it and they forced themselves to speak it. Some while eating sushi arranged on a large, slightly rounded, rectangular tray, others while partaking of the homemade carrot salad that filled a cherry wood bowl. Still others communicated in French seated around a plate of cheeses and a big lacquer platter filled with bread, the two dishes placed next to each other on a little round table made of glass. As for me, leaning against the traditional-style chest of drawers of a deep maple colour that stood in the corner close to the glass door of the living room, I was having a discussion with my ex-banker friend as I poured him some of the Italian red he'd brought himself.

It was at that point that I heard distinctly plaintive little cries, a series of moans coming from my study. I could also recognise amid the voices and the softly playing background music the sharp little sounds that Mélodie made when scratching on the door. I'd taken the step of shutting her in my study before the guests arrived so that the evening wouldn't be disturbed by the kind of canine exuberance that was not always universally appreciated. She could hear voices, other voices than those she was used to, laughing voices, voices that rose up at times like musical notes played *fortissimo*. The same little sounds were repeated; the same plaintive cries, closer and closer together, went on longer before stopping suddenly after a brief, stifled bark. She was clearly protesting about the treatment that had been inflicted on her, being forcibly separated from those who were happily adding their voices to mine and my wife's and my daughter's. Her voice howling and her paws knocking at the door, she expressed her desire to meet us beyond an invisible divide that separated her from the human community.

Her sorrowful moans pained me. I addressed the gathering.

'Good evening, I bid you all welcome! I'm so happy that you're here. But ... there's something I have to say if I'm to be perfectly frank with you. Even though this evening has got off to such a good start there's something stopping me from really enjoying it. As we stand here there's a being somewhere else in this house who is in distress ... That soft moaning sound? Can you hear it?'

All at once the voices gave way to the background music that subtly filled the apartment. I lowered the volume. There was silence. Then we heard little moans like the delicate twittering of birds or, rather, the sad, lingering sound of a flute coming from the wings of a concert hall. In the end they elicited a scattering of broad smiles on the faces of the guests.

'When she sees this happy throng she'll be very excited at first, but she'll calm down quite quickly and enjoy being part of it all. Can I let her come in and join you?'

No one was allergic to dog hair, no one was afraid of this other living creature not quite like us. I went to open the door of my study. She was sitting on her back legs. She looked at me for a long time; she was trembling with impatience.

'Are you coming?'

Scarcely had she heard the first syllable of my signal than she leapt forward in one bound. Three seconds later she was scurrying about in the forest of legs and running madly from one person to another before lying on her back, her legs in the air in front of the Haitian poet, who knew exactly how to deal with this exuberant ball of energy ready to lavish you with affection. Mélodie's tension relaxed. When she stood up again she gave the poet her front paws in turn as if to thank her for her pats. Then she went off, as naturally as could be, to lie on her dining room mattress. No doubt reassured by the presence of humans nearby, she soon began dozing.

The voices rose up again, intermingling. And the music, muted and lilting, was now playing again as well, just lightly perceptible to our ears. The party went on till late. No one wanted to take their leave of any of the others. In the end there was nothing left to eat or drink. On the table there was only a large carafe of water in the shape of a stork, like the magic fountain at an ancient festival where young lovers would come to quench their thirst. The guests, in little groups of two or three whose composition changed from time to time, gossiped animatedly and in every corner. As for me, with the concern appropriate to the inspirer of this motley gathering of a winter's evening, I went from one group to another as if to form them into a joyfully woven whole.

It was at that moment, when no one was expecting it, that there appeared a most unusual sight. Mélodie, who up until then had been sleeping on her mattress, got up suddenly and came and stood right in the middle of the living room. Crouching down in front of her, I took her right front paw in the way I usually did and said to her,

'What's going on, my friend? Are you coming to take part in our gathering?'

The voices grew quiet. All eyes, in a kind of childlike wonder, converged on the one who'd just taken up a spot among us. The eyes of the dog, wide open, shining, with a disarming candour, looked all around her as if checking the presence of those she'd noted a few hours before. With that she rested her head on her two paws, giving a deep sigh.

Someone burst out laughing. A woman's voice said,

'It might be time to go off to bed ...'

This remark, which was doubtless addressed to Mélodie, was enough to remind us that time had slipped by without our realising it, in the absence of a reason to think of it. It was true; we did have to go our separate ways.

There was getting up to go. Belongings were gathered up and visits were made to the little room next to the bathroom. Goodbyes were said in the hall. There was hugging. Shoes were put back on. There was more hugging. Finally the exit was made. But instead of dispersing, we gathered again in front of the house, quite naturally, without anyone prompting us to do so. A whispered conversation was struck up for a few seconds. Then we went our separate ways. The wind had swept away all the clouds. The city was plunged into the silence of the night. The moon, silvery, almost white, in the infinitely high and starry sky shone its light on the men and women who were gradually moving further into the distance and coupled them with a faithful shadow. We went back into the house.

Mélodie was sleeping at the foot of our bed.

20

WAITING

SHE WAITS. Mélodie is one who waits, who does nothing but wait. Her life will have been made up of waiting. But waiting for what? Waiting for the return of the one to whom she feels attached.

That morning, as usual, I had taken her for a walk and, after a long stroll through the laneways of Nakano, we made a stop at Philosophy Park before getting back to the house. Once the passers-by thinned out in the vacant land adjoining the park, I was in the habit of taking off her leash so that she could freely explore the area in her own way, from end to end and in every nook and cranny. So that's what I did. I knew that if, say, a child was frightened by her presence I only needed to call loudly to her, and she would come straight back to me. But that day things took a different turn.

Mr D, the vet, came along with his female golden retriever, Momo—he would regularly get her to chase the frisbee.

ABSOLUTE FIDELITY: TO WAIT TILL IT KILLS YOU

I greeted him and thanked him for looking after Mélodie two weeks before when she'd had a split dewclaw. The greetings over with, I turned round to the ex-patient. But I could no longer see her ... She had disappeared ... She had fled—that's what I guessed straight away—as soon as she'd seen the man who had hurt her so dreadfully—he'd cut away half of her broken dewclaw together with the nerve that ran underneath it. I cried out her name. Now there were only Mr D and his dog on the vacant land. I took my leave of the vet and ran into the different parts of the park, shouting, screaming her name louder and louder: I looked around by the baseball stadium; I checked the area around the tennis courts; I also searched the cherry-tree garden; finally I continued the search as far as the pagoda and its surrounds. But in vain. Not the shadow of a dog. I was beginning to panic ...

'Mélodie! Mélodie! Where are you? Come back, please come back! Mélodie!'

So there I was, dashing around frantically, looking in all the out-of-the-way corners of the park where a lovable dog, all atremble, might be hiding. In my right hand I held the red leash, and in the left, the little walks bag containing the bottle of water and some advertising liftouts. I was hot. I was bathed in sweat; big drops of perspiration ran down my cheeks and down my back the whole length of my spine. I looked at my watch. It was past ten o'clock. That meant we should have been home more than an hour ago. I was exhausted. I sighed despondently.

It was then that a woman in her forties, who was holding a Shiba on the leash, spoke to me. Seeing me in the state of panic that showed I was a master looking for his dog, in this highly visible state of distress, no doubt she felt sorry for me:

'Are you looking for your dog? I don't know if it's yours, but there's a dog over there, on the footpath, near the entrance.'

'What does it look like? Is it a big dog? Is it a golden retriever?'

'Yes, it is, it's a golden retriever. It was sitting, looking towards the entrance ... It looked like it was waiting ...'

'Thank you, madam.'

Having stammered these few words of thanks, I strode off at once. I headed straight for the exit. 'Oh, so you'd decided to go back home, you little rascal!' I said to myself. 'Well, I didn't think of that!' I arrived at the exit, I hurtled down the stairs, I leapt onto the footpath of Nakano Avenue. And yes, there I found the frightened runaway. She was sitting on her back legs, straight as a rod. As soon as she saw me, she bowed her head forward a little, as if she was embarrassed and felt a sudden rush of uneasiness.

'You were *waiting* for me here! I didn't know! Oh, I'm sorry. How long have you been waiting for me? I've been looking for you for an hour. Which means you've been here for an hour waiting for me? Is that right? Oh, I should have thought of that! Useless as ever!'

She got up and stood on her four legs. Then she grabbed me with all her strength between her two front legs and began to moan softly.

'Yes ... it's OK. It's OK, Mélodie.'

Then she resumed her sitting position, all the time looking up at me. I knelt down; I took Mélodie's head in both hands and I said to her, 'I feel reassured again now. Thank you a thousand times over.'

I clasped her in my arms; I pressed my cheek against hers. She did the same to me, licking me furiously. Eventually though, her elaborate displays of affection came to an end. I got up and attached the leash to her collar. We made our way from Philosophy Park. From time to time the sun clouded over. The breeze rustled the soft green leaves of the cherry trees and brushed gently over my forehead.

Suddenly I felt cold.

Mélodie waits. She waits, for example, with the patience of a Tibetan monk before starting the meal that has been prepared for her. I am not one of those people who make their dog wait because they like making it wait. I don't share their enjoyment in such futile contortions that only satisfy the rather sadistic pride of the master. But one day it happened that, quite unwittingly, I made Mélodie wait more than three quarters of an hour in front of her well-filled dish.

Just as I was about to say, 'Go on, eat!' the telephone rang. I ran to the living room to pick up the receiver. It was an old lady of more than eighty, a neighbour who lived by herself, who was calling me to ask for help. She told me that she needed to replace the blown globes of her ceiling lights; that there was now only one that worked; that she was really afraid of finding herself in the dark one evening; that her son, who usually saw to it, could no longer do it because he had recently moved and now he lived too far away; that she'd bought the globes herself now, the same ones. Finally, she was brave enough to ask me if it wasn't too much trouble for me to come and put them in, because she was so afraid of falling when she was getting up on the step-ladder. I told her that it wasn't any trouble at all for me and that I was coming over straight away to help her get it all done.

Her little wooden house is two minutes' walk from ours. Equipped with a few tools, I set off without delay. I get to her place and get busy getting the ceiling lights working again. Undo the cover, replace the blown bulbs, put back the cover: it was all fixed in twenty minutes. As a token of thanks the old lady offered me a cup of tea with a delicious little cake. 'Really, you shouldn't be embarrassed. When you need a globe replaced you call me, Mrs Satoh! OK? You've seen how easy it is for me? How many days have you been here with just the light from one globe? … Be reasonable, Mrs Satoh! Next time call me straight away. Promise? …'

And so the conversation continued over the pleasant aroma of green tea, which blended with the heady scent of the old house.

Then, the sound of garbage collectors in the street …

Suddenly I remembered that I hadn't yet fed Mélodie. 'I'm sorry, Mrs Satoh, I have to go back. I've left Mélodie at home on her own; I've got things to do, I'm sorry…'

I run. I go up the stairs in a flash. I open the door; I stagger as I take off my shoes; I rush to the kitchen where I'd abandoned her.

What do I see?

Mélodie was lying next to her untouched food bowl. She was waiting.

'I'm sorry, Mélodie. I'd completely forgotten about you! I'm not a fit and proper master! I feel dreadful!'

She got up straight away and sat on her haunches. She hadn't touched her meal, which had turned into a sort of chestnut purée. With a patience that had conquered her desire to satisfy her appetite while she sat looking at her food, clearly she was waiting for us to resume our ritual of 'civility', doubtless quite imaginary, but that had the virtue of shaping our life, of imparting a certain rhythm to our daily gestures and, especially, of softening and smoothing our relations and therefore of eliminating from them any element of coarseness and lack of delicacy.

Dogs, unlike wolves, are animals that have been domesticated for more than ten thousand years. They were the first animal to be domesticated, says Alexandra Horowitz, author of *Inside of a Dog*. 'Domesticated' means that mankind and the society of which it is at once the cause and effect play an important part in the very construction of this animal being. The control over desire (appetite), to which this wait of three quarters of an hour bears witness, shows that, for Mélodie, nature bows before an imprint of a cultural order that stems from the alliance of humans and dogs over ten millennia.

The longest wait that Mélodie endured was that of the first of January, leaving aside the one that we regularly inflicted on her each time we left for France in summer.

The New Year's Day celebration is one that brings together the members of the family who are scattered in different places during the rest of the year. It is one of the occasions on which, with incontrovertible authority, the power of the family unit to give structure and form to the lives of its members is made manifest. Under no circumstances could one fail to take part in it.

We are in the habit of spending the evening of 31 December with my elderly mother, who lives in Tsurukawa, still in Tokyo, but, even so, more than thirty-five kilometres from our place, to welcome in together, in the invigorating cold of the depths of night, the very first moments of the new year. A little before midnight we will go to a Buddhist temple nearby and, there, with a little wooden hammer, we ring 108 little bells hanging beneath the roof of a gallery that leads to the main shrine. According to tradition, within a man there dwell 108 evil desires that he must drive out before he begins the new year. This takes ten minutes. After the bell-ringing we go and see a very old priest, probably the highest dignitary of the temple, who gives us a quick tap on the right shoulder with a sacred text more than ten centimetres thick. When this ceremony is completed we are served very hot sweet sake. My mother, slightly stooped, gives me her arm so that I can support her while, slowly and carefully, we make our way. On the little pathway separating the shrine from the gallery of bells there are men stoking a big fire around which the sometime pilgrims warm themselves for a moment before going off to have their first dream of the year.

It's a habit that I have taken up again since the death of Mélodie in 2009. When she was with us it was impossible for us to spend the night of New Year's Eve in the way I've described, following this little ritual of ours. I could of course have taken Mélodie to my mother's, and in fact I once did, but I couldn't bear seeing her in the entry hall, tied up to the base of the shoe stand. Neither my mother nor my brother's family who live next door could get used to the unwonted animal intrusion. It was by definition disturbing and unclean. Her presence among them was not wanted; I saw it at once. Because of that I preferred to spend the night of 31 December away from my mother, with Mélodie. So on the morning of the first day of the new year we'd get up very early to go and partake ceremoniously of the first breakfast of the year, which my mother had carefully prepared according to the traditional rules of her country.

We would leave around half past seven. Seeing us busy getting ready to go, Mélodie would be unsettled. She'd keep at my heels, watching my every movement. When everything was ready I'd ask Michèle and Julia-Madoka to go out first and wait for me in the car. Mélodie would place herself at the entrance, sitting on her haunches. I spoke to her, kneeling in front of her, 'You'll be spending a long day at home on your own. I'd really like to take you with us. But we can't. You wouldn't be happy there. There are people there who can't really accept you because you're not like us … We'll be back this evening. And we'll have our walk … a bit late, but it'll be the same as usual … All right, Mélodie, goodbye, till this evening. *Gomen ne, Mélodie-chan*' (*chan* placed after a first name signifies great affection in relation to the child who bears it; the translation of this phrase would be something like: I'm sorry, my dear little Mélodie).

I'd close the door very softly; Mélodie's eyes, imploring, disappeared into the space of the door as it closed. I'd leave, with death in my heart.

WAITING

Not everything stops on the first of January, but the slowing down of normal activity is obvious. Only the more grasping businesses, always ready to rob mindless customers, the consumer addicts, stay open. I enjoy cruising along the almost deserted motorway admiring, when it's fine—and it often is on New Year's Day—Fuji-san in the perfect clarity of a winter's day. When we get to my mother's we greet her as well as my brother and his family more solemnly than usual, with set words and expressions used only on that day. Before we sit down at the table I spend a moment of quiet reflection standing in front of the family altar on which is placed the little wooden funerary stele bearing the Buddhist name of my father. I close my eyes, and, in the darkness of the silent space thus created within me, I call on the soul of my father, who died in 1994. I present to him the projects I am to undertake in the coming year.

Like my father, and my mother and brother, I am a man without religion. My father, who, in a childhood of crushing poverty, had been a trainee monk, deplored the industrial form that the Buddhist religion had come to take in modern Japanese society, while at the same time retaining a sense of the sacred and attributing a transcendental value to prayer. His aversion to the business of death was such that when his own father and mother died he took it upon himself to compose their Buddhist names—the knowledge that his religious education had given him allowed him to do this— names that are ordinarily purchased at exorbitant cost when using the services offered by a firm of undertakers. And so, he had prevented my brother and me from calling on a religious functionary at the time of his own death. In our family, for funeral rites, there has never been any religious ceremony and certainly no Buddhist priest in attendance. The ceremony, if ceremony it is, is simply a moment of intense remembrance of the deceased by his loved ones. The minutes of reflection that I give myself standing before the little shrine set into the wall of my mother's bedroom, free from any worry about correct form, are therefore devoid of any religious undertones.

The breakfast consists of a soup filled with a rich assortment of ingredients—*mochi* (balls of sticky rice), chicken, bamboo shoots, herbs—and of several small dishes whose names bring to mind the wishes for health and prosperity which the ancestors of the archipelago made long ago. My mother opens the proceedings and wishes that we may all enjoy good health, mutual kindness and success in our work and studies. Next, we take it in turns to share our plans, while praising the talents of she who has devoted herself to the preparation of the breakfast.

The end of this morning meal, a real feast, is the beginning of a long day that follows a set pattern. There is not a great deal to do other than have a walk, which takes us to two temples, one Shinto, the other Buddhist (different from that of the 108 bells), two places that are particularly tranquil in keeping with the serenity we seek that day. I make the most of this walk of an hour and a half in which I take my mother's left arm in my right and keep our arms firmly linked, just to be able to chat with her about this and that. I'm especially eager to spend time with her like this since I haven't been able to accompany her the previous day for the ritual of ringing the 108 bells driving out the same number of evil desires ...

Once she is back home, my mother, helped by her two daughters-in-law, busies herself with dinner, for which she has asked her fishmonger to prepare a fine array of sashimi and her butcher to cut several slices of beef of excellent quality. My brother splurges on a bottle of champagne, and I do likewise, although I don't have a drop of it: in three hours' time I'll be driving home again (when I'm driving I make this a strict rule, knowing that half a glass of beer makes my violinist brother lose the perfect control of his fingers).

Dinner goes on into the night hours, but on the stroke of ten I announce that we have to go home as it's getting late. The long day of the first of January concludes with repeated thanks and the promise, at once vague and sincere, to get together again soon.

It's past eleven when we get home. The car stops. The gate of the car park, activated by remote control, opens slowly, making a metallic clinking like the grinding of teeth.

The sound of the engine revving and then suddenly stopping. The sound of car doors being closed, like sharp, muffled explosions ... Then voices back and forth ...

Mélodie, her muzzle resting on her two front legs, submerged in the half-light of the study, right next to my chair, instantly pricks up her ears.

The sound of footsteps coming up the stairs.

She leaps up and goes straight into the hall. She waits.

At last I get to the door. I put the first key into the lock at the top, then the second into the lock at the bottom.

At last the door opens. A man's shadow appears. It moves forward and goes into the hall.

'How are you, my friend? We're back late. Forgive us. Today's a bit special. But it's over! We're home again!'

Mélodie would be standing on her back legs and trying to grab me with her front ones, to put them around me, as she liked to do. She was almost as tall as me; she'd manage to lick my face. While she was putting her front legs back on the floor and starting to lavish me with affection all over again, I'd put my things down and turn on the lights in the hall. When I squatted down on my heels she'd roll over on to her back, making little moans of joy, and uninhibitedly reveal her pinkish-white belly to me. I'd stroke her along the full length of it. And so, softly, softly, calm would return …

But one year something quite unexpected happened and rather upset the ritual of our homecoming reunion on New Year's Day. When I stroked Mélodie lying stretched out on her back she suddenly turned back over and jumped straight up, making a getaway movement, as if she had no wish to stay where she was …

A little pool of yellow liquid had appeared on the wooden floor. It reminded me of my fright at seeing the reddish urine …

She'd been waiting for our return for fourteen hours. Bursting with joy, the certainty of no longer being abandoned was more than enough to make her lose control of her bladder. That was quite normal. Little children everywhere will wet their pants when, bursting with infantile exuberance, their father tickles them in a Sunday-evening game.

'Do you want to go for a walk?'

As soon as I opened the door she rushed out on to the balcony and, reassured that I was following her, went down the stairs as fast as she could. Once out in the street she went straight to her own little spot on the big thoroughfare of Nakano Avenue. She could finally relieve herself and was freed from the prison of that interminable fourteen-hour wait that I'd inflicted on her. She walked three metres ahead of me off the leash, almost skipping sometimes. It was getting late. Now and then cars drove past. A man in a suit was quickening his steps to get home. A couple of young late-night revellers were walking on the opposite footpath, beneath the thick branches of the bare cherry trees. The laughter of the woman echoed in the night.

Now I could give myself up to the pleasure of finally being able to respond to Mélodie's unfailing fidelity; for a long time I strolled along with her at my side through the city lying deep in sleep.

Diary Extract 5

**Fragments that Have Slipped from
the Notebook of a Dog's Companion**

Once there was a dog that was changed into a statue for having *waited* in the same place, at the same time, in an immutable and always identical position. He was called Hachiko (or Hachi, as a kind of diminutive). He was an Akita, a dog that came from the department of Akita in the province of Tōhoku.

On 14 January 1924 an Akita puppy had been sent from the mountainous hinterland of Akita to the house of Hidesaburō Ueno, a professor of agronomy at the Imperial University of Tokyo, who lived in the district of Shibuya in Tokyo. The puppy travelled more than twenty hours by train to get to Ueno's station. Hidesaburo gave him the name Hachi and began to feel a deep affection for the animal. He took the train at Shibuya Station to go and work at the university, and Hachi would often go with him to the station. But a year and a few months after Hachi had come to Professor Ueno's house the professor died suddenly. It was 21 May 1925. He had taken the train as usual at Shibuya. Hachi had gone with him as usual.

DIARY EXTRACT 5

That evening, at the time his master returned, Hachi, faithfully at his post, waited for him at the station exit. But Professor Ueno did not reappear. He had died at the university, as a result of a brain haemorrhage. Hachi did not give up his vigil; he stayed at the station until late. But when night fell he went back home. People went about preparing for the funeral in a state of general upheaval. For Hachi this separation was too brutal, beyond his understanding. Well away from the scrutiny of the men and women who kept bustling about, he went on looking for his master and everything that was a reminder of him. At last, in a dark little corner of the big house, he found some things that belonged to him. He remained there glued to them for three days without eating.

The house was sold. Mrs Ueno, who was not legally the wife of Hidesaburo, had no right to the estate. She had no other choice, to survive, than to return to the place where she was born, to her own people. As for Hachi, she was not in a position to take him with her, and he was entrusted to a cloth merchant of whom she was a distant relative. But he was soon sent away on the pretext that he jumped up on the customers and frightened them. He was then handed over into the care of other people: he went from suburb to suburb, from house to house. No arrangement was really a happy one. And all the while Hachi did not stop thinking about his missing master. He ran away more and more frequently. He would often pass by the old house of the Ueno family to see if his master had returned, but most often he went to the station of Shibuya at the end of the day to see if he was among the passengers leaving the station. Some of those who worked at the station, accustomed to him being there regularly, no longer shooed him away. The man who sold chicken skewers from his mobile shop next to the exit marvelled at the dog's faithfulness and befriended him. He would regularly give him something to eat.

ABSOLUTE FIDELITY: TO WAIT TILL IT KILLS YOU

Day after day, month after month, went by like this. And, in the monotonous regularity of city life, almost ten years passed without a single day going by that Hachi did not take up his position at the exit to the station. Always in the same place, always at the same time, always in the same position (namely sitting, his attentive gaze fixed on the ticket gate), he waited tirelessly, indefatigably, inexhaustibly for Professor Ueno. And during that time the gap inexorably widened between Hachi's rapidly aging body and his inner image of his master, which did not age at all. Finally that gap could grow no wider. Time swept everything away, obliterated everything. Hachi gave up the ghost on 8 March 1935 in a Shibuya laneway situated on the other side of the station, a part of town he rarely used to visit.

Beating away somewhere in my adult's sixty-year-old body there is the heart of a child, which is moved by the tale of this dog and his absolute fidelity. Something that is very ancient, no doubt, which goes beyond the context of recollections and individual memories, is awoken in us by this story. You feel the need to preserve its imprint and to make it tangible. Hachi's stuffed body is now to be found in the Museum of Agronomy of the University of Tokyo, where Professor Ueno had taught, while his flesh and bones, reduced to ashes, lie in the cemetery of Aoyama alongside the remains of his master. Hachi's body, in another way, has been petrified so as to undergo no further change. At Shibuya station, unrecognisable today because of its vastness and the mass of people who pass through it and swarm around it day and night, there is now a statue of a dog sitting on its hind legs: in a position of waiting. There are always a great many people, young and not so

DIARY EXTRACT 5

young, hailing from different cultural and geographic backgrounds, who have taken up their positions around Hachi thus immortalised in bronze, and who themselves are waiting for those they are meeting there. When I go to this part of town, which is now one of the liveliest and busiest shopping areas of Tokyo, and where, ultimately, people do no more than just pass through, I am seized by a strange feeling of disquiet, doubtless due to the contradiction, crystallised around the statue, between the infinite waiting of the faithful dog and the ephemeral moment of the meetings of the passers-by and the passengers engaged in perpetual and never repeated movements.

The fact remains that we love Hachi's story as we love our long-gone childhood, an enchanted world that has disappeared forever, the truth of another time dimension, like the founding myth of a beautiful, forgotten country whose distant memory we have nevertheless retained. The story is so well loved in fact that two films have been made about it: firstly, *Hachi-ko* by Seijirō Kōyama, from 1987. Then a remake of it in 2009 by the American director Lasse Hallström, *Hachi: A Dog's Tale*. I don't think that they're masterpieces from a cinematographic point of view. But in both films I find the poignant contrast (or perhaps simply the idea of that contrast) between the shortness of the life of the dog and the infinite waiting that he is able to take on quite shattering.

To wait is to believe in the other's return. Hachi did nothing but wait for his master's return. He believed in his return. Clearly he was unable to see Professor Ueno, but that extraordinary and incredible capacity for waiting convinces me that Hachi had a kind of unalterable inner vision of his master. If not, why wait? Why use all the time remaining to him in waiting? I think I understand why the two filmmakers felt the need, at the end of their films, to have the ghost return. Some will criticise them for it, accusing them of cheap sentimentality. I can understand their viewpoint, but it's not one I share.

Hachi was not fortunate enough to see his master again. But Argus did. The famous episode in the *Odyssey* of Ulysses' dog is one we are all familiar with. Roger Grenier quotes it at the beginning of his fine book, *The Difficulty of Being a Dog*. J-B Pontalis also talks about it in *Elles*, when he describes his recollections of his dog, Oreste. I in turn cannot resist the pleasure of presenting this central moment. Ulysses, or Odysseus, King of Ithaca, returns. After twenty years away he reaches his island, disguised as a miserable old beggar. Only his dog Argus recognises him, and dies then and there.

> Stretched on the ground close to where they stood talking [Odysseus and Eumaeus the swineherd], there lay a dog, who now pricked up his ears and raised his head. Argus was his name. Odysseus himself had owned and trained him, though he had sailed for holy Ilium before he could reap the reward of his patience ... There, full of vermin, lay Argus the hound. But directly he became aware of Odysseus' presence, he wagged his tail and dropped his ears, though he lacked the strength now to come any nearer to his master. Yet Odysseus saw him out of the corner of his eye, and brushed a tear away ... As for Argus, he had no sooner set eyes on Odysseus after those nineteen years than he succumbed to the black hand of death.[*]

Argus's longevity surprises me. Hachi only lived for thirteen years; Mélodie for twelve years and three months. Ulysses' dog waited

---

[*] Homer, *The Odyssey*, trans. EV Riev.

DIARY EXTRACT 5

for his master for twenty years; Hachi for almost ten years. That 'black hand of death' that suddenly followed the reappearance of his master is telling about the emotion that overwhelmed the old dog. It was as if he lived on his waiting, as a source of desire and of vital energy. What were the last moments of Hachi's life like, in that sad Shibuya alley? At the back of his eyes, on that dark inner screen, did he see Professor Ueno returning? Did he see his ghost? How did life, so nonchalant and cruel, leave Hachi's body? As for Mélodie, happily, she didn't experience such a torture of waiting. Still, wasn't she waiting for me—because that is in fact what she was doing, as short as the wait was—the evening of 2 December 2009, before she gave up her last breath?

But what, more than anything else, moves me so deeply each time that I return in the *Odyssey* to the scene of Argus's discreet reunion with Ulysses is the fact that his appearance, his outward form as a miserable old beggar, which makes him unrecognisable to human eyes, has absolutely no influence over the attitude and attachment of Argus. What the old dog sees in Ulysses, whether he is a king or a beggar, is his being, after his historically constituted or artificially constructed outward appearance has been stripped from him. That alone is what Argus perceives. Ulysses' being, to which only Argus is sensitive, makes me think of the statue of which Rousseau speaks in the *Discourse on Inequality*, that of Glaucus, 'which time, the sea and storms had so disfigured that it was more like a wild beast than a god'.

In the Nazi death camps the prisoners as we know were no longer considered human beings; their status was that of commodities, and as a result their persecutors referred to them, and addressed them, by a number. How had they come to that? In the system of the concentration camps, as unlikely as it may seem, the Nazi torturers had lost the ability to see humanity on (or underneath) a person's face. According to Emmanuel Levinas, who recalls his memories of Bobby in 'The Name of a Dog, or Natural Rights', it was just this stray dog who could recognise the prisoners' humanity:

> The other men, described as free, who came into contact with us or who gave us work or orders or even a smile—and the children and the women who passed by and who, sometimes, would lift their eyes to look at us—stripped us of our human skin, we were only a kind of quasi-humanity, a troop of monkeys ...
>
> And then, around the middle of a long period of captivity ... a stray dog happens to come into our lives. One day he came and joined the motley crew when, under guard, it was returning from work. He managed to survive somehow in some wild corner in the vicinity of the camp. But we called him Bobby, an exotic name, as befitting an adored dog. He turned up at the morning assemblies and would be waiting for us on our return. Jumping about and barking gaily. For him—there was no question about it—we were men.

This headspinning realisation: humanity denied by men but felt and shared by an animal.

One day on television, a report about Berlin's policy regarding the protection of dogs showed a homeless young woman of about thirty who had two magnificent big dogs. The thirty-year-old woman—she looked twenty years older—was a former drug addict who had come out of it thanks to the responsibility, the word she herself chose, that she took on in relation to her dogs. She said that she was fulfilling her duty as a citizen in paying the municipal tax for the dogs and that she spent half of her income on feeding her companions. As she answered the interviewer's questions she radiated a certain kind of beauty and that special glow that comes from having regained one's health. The two dogs, sitting impassively at her side and supremely indifferent to the stares of the passers-by who hurried along glancing furtively at the *ménage à trois*, were as handsome as athletes of ancient Greece in full possession of their strength.

Hachi, turned to stone, made into a statue, lives at the very heart of the mad urban bustle of Tokyo, as a symbol of *absolute fidelity*, of an unwavering attachment, of an indestructible love, unattainable for the unhappy humans, in essence, as a memory of an elysian world lost forever, like the two lovers in the *The Devil's Envoys* (1942)—Gilles and Anne—who are turned to stone and whose hearts, triumphing over time, keep on beating.

Part III

'YOU ASK THAT I FORGET YOU? FEAR NOT, MY BELOVED.'

(WOLFGANG AMADEUS MOZART, K 505)

21

TO WAKE OR NOT TO WAKE?

ONE SUMMER NIGHT during the holidays of 2005, Mélodie, who was no longer a young dog, was sleeping as usual at my feet in our bedroom. I say 'at my feet' because I'd stayed in Tokyo on my own, while Michèle and Julia-Madoka went to France for a month so that Michèle could see her elderly mother again and Julia-Madoka could experience French life both among family and socially. The heat and humidity that had penetrated the bedroom did not yield to the cool air mutely circulating through the apartment thanks to the air-conditioning. I had gone to bed early so that I could rise early. There was no question of walking Mélodie in the heat of the bitumened streets, blazing hot after eight o'clock in the morning.

I've been a light sleeper since the birth of my daughter. I'd acquired the habit, unwittingly, of sleeping very lightly so that I could get up at the slightest sound coming from the baby's bedroom. The open doors of the bedrooms, hers and

'YOU ASK THAT I FORGET YOU? FEAR NOT, MY BELOVED.'

ours, meant that we could respond to the little girl whenever she called out and go to her—if we needed to—in a flash. Julia-Madoka having now grown up, her place was taken by Mélodie, who of course was not growing up in the same sense. I'd become attuned to all the nocturnal signals made by this elderly infant.

That night the heat, really quite unbearable, was causing me discomfort. I had over me neither a blanket nor sheets, but the ambient heat, close to my body temperature, had first warmed the mattress before assailing me on all sides. I was like a fish thrashing around on a hotplate. I couldn't get to sleep. Nonetheless, before dawn, I'd disappeared into the folds of night, and it was the first glimmers of day, still quite pale, that little by little prised me from sleep. It must have been about half past four. I heard the sharp little noise made by Mélodie's claws on the wooden floor, which meant that she was suddenly getting up for some reason I tried to identify. Was she suffering from the heat as I was? Very likely, as this humid, oppressive heat was no doubt unheard of in Scotland, the country of origin of the golden retriever. Was she going to have a drink from her bowl, which was always left in the kitchen at the other end of the apartment? I was listening for her movement, my hearing still only half awake. She took just a few steps and flopped down as if to go to sleep again. She could doubtless no longer bear being on the floor where it had become burning hot from contact with her outstretched body, and wanted a cool spot, if possible exposed to the slight draught coming from the fanlight of the entry hall.

But, a few moments later, Mélodie got up and started moving purposefully towards me. Then she stopped dead.

A silence broken by panting. She was completely still. Then she started to walk again. In my state of semi-sleep, I was aware of the sheer weight of my closed eyelids. Even so, my attention was turned towards the dog, sensing her hesitant concentration. Finally she made up her mind and came closer to me. Her warm, heavy breath brushed my forehead. Gradually I emerged from my summer sleep. But I kept pretending to be asleep, turning on to my left side. Was she trying to tell me that she was ready for a good long walk? I was expecting her tongue to lick me to wake me up. I could still feel her warm, heavy breath, which had just tickled my face.

But no, Mélodie didn't lick me. Ten centimetres from my cheek, she sniffed my salty perspiration; her tongue, pink and moist, was hanging out and was on the verge of touching my skin. But, at the last minute, she refrained from licking me. She preferred to let me sleep a little longer. I don't know how she came to this decision to resist doing what she wanted to do. She knew how to say to me things like, 'Well, isn't it time for our walk?' When I found it difficult to tear myself away from my computer screen because of a sentence I couldn't get right, Mélodie would come up to me with her head tilted, questioning, urging me to come. But that morning, although her temptation to wake me up was pushed to the limit, she didn't give in to it. She decided to leave me in peace; that much was clear.

The following year something occurred that was both similar and dissimilar. In autumn 2006 the political tension was gradually rising in France in light of the presidential election of April–May 2007. Far from the Hexagon, I was still paying attention to what was going to happen with the Socialists in their presidential primary.

Opposing Laurent Fabius and Dominique Strauss-Kahn, the latter still alive on the political scene, an elegant woman was positioning herself to contest the presidency of the Republic. In a European country like France, with its long patriarchal tradition, wasn't the smiling presence of Ségolène Royal in a cohort of political men an event in itself? To me in any case it seemed to be the culmination of a certain historical process and at the same time the sign of a change that was starting to penetrate deeply into the social fabric. Finally, on 26 November, at the Socialist Party's extraordinary Congress of nomination, the victory of Ségolène Royal was officially proclaimed. The Socialist candidate for the presidential election was then to deliver her nomination speech. What would she say when facing the men who'd been set aside and who might not be able to rid themselves of a certain secret frustration despite their jubilant mien? Over meals Michèle and I spent a lot of time talking about the emergence of a woman Socialist candidate for the presidency and therefore of the real possibility of a woman president of the Republic, which, beyond what that implied in our profession as teachers of French abroad, had considerable significance at the other end of the world where a Minister of Health brazenly dared to say that, when it came down to it, women were only machines for giving birth.

In Tokyo—which is eight hours ahead of France in winter—if you wanted to listen to Ségolène Royal live over the internet you had to get up in the middle of the night. I decided against it given my to-do list the following day. The speech would be published at length. You would be able to download it; it would be available in its entirety on YouTube. So despite the temptation to wait up, we went to bed at a reasonable hour.

A few hours later I was woken by a little restlessness on the part of Mélodie, who'd got up suddenly. She came up to me and sat on her back legs. I just wanted to stay hidden away in sleep, taking refuge in the night, and my response was to burrow down even further under the futon. But she persisted. She didn't back off. Instead she came close and leant over my head, which was emerging from the futon. Finally she licked her master's cheek with her rough tongue as if to force him out of his hiding place.

'What's the matter, Mélodie? It's too early …'

I turned on the bedside light. It was after three … The dog was there, wide awake, her head tilting perceptibly to the left, questioning, as she would often do at times like that …

'Ah, Ségolène …'

I leapt out of bed and turned on my computer. I don't remember now which site I went to. In any case I was able to listen live to Ségolène Royal's speech, which, among other things, drew the attention of the listeners to the historical significance of the female candidature for the office of president, while recalling the landmarks in the history of women since Olympe de Gouges.

During all the time that I turned my ear to this ever so slightly nasal voice, perhaps prematurely tinged with a fatal fragility, Mélodie, supremely peaceful, stayed near me, her

> 'YOU ASK THAT I FORGET YOU? FEAR NOT, MY BELOVED.'

eyes closed, her muzzle resting on my left foot. Throughout her life of twelve years and three months, she woke me on several occasions at unaccustomed times, but each time was either to tell me about a physical discomfort she was suffering from or to alert me to some emergency I had to deal with. That night it was neither of those. She had detected in me a desire, an expectation—but how? that is the unfathomable thing that bound me to this animal—in relation to a political speech that could stir the conscience in a society very far from the place of its delivery, a society structured in a way that is essentially homosocial. For how else are we to understand Mélodie's strange nocturnal greeting?

22

EAT ME!

IT IS NOW more than 850 days since Mélodie died; my father passed away eighteen years ago. Shadows—sometimes like the animal and sometimes like the man—move through my dreams. Mere wraiths now, Mélodie and my father stubbornly return in the world of my nights. They are like crutches on which I lean to go forward; they are like blazing torches that reconcile me to the spreading gloom.

I was lying on the ground on a black rug in a little room I didn't recognise, a room without furniture, windows or doors, far from any human habitation. The bare walls were of wood, chalet-style. I wasn't wounded; I wasn't suffering. My body was there, whole. It belonged to me. But I was dead. I felt that I was dead. Or rather, alive, I was already in the skin of

'YOU ASK THAT I FORGET YOU? FEAR NOT, MY BELOVED.'

someone who was dead—and that someone was me. Silence reigned. Even so, I could hear Mélodie's little footsteps. She had stayed there, with me. All the others had disappeared from my horizon. Mélodie was my sole companion in this enclosed space, which was clearly forgotten by the rest of the world. Sometimes she stood up on her back legs; sometimes she came right up to me to stand over me: her head, above me, was watching me; her muzzle sniffed my face; now and then her tongue licked my cheek. In this way time seemed to slip by without reckoning.

But all of a sudden the scene darkened, and I was struck by Mélodie having become excessively thin. I was dead and there was no one but me with her. No one was feeding her. No one was looking after her. And I couldn't do anything, because I was dead. With nothing to eat Mélodie kept getting thinner. Sad, powerless, I saw that she was becoming visibly weaker. Her coat, which had been pure-white, was now a brownish colour.

Starving and emaciated, Mélodie painfully put one foot in front of another. I could hear her hesitant footsteps, spaced out and irregular. She came to see me nevertheless, and she repeated the same gestures: she watched me from above, she sniffed my face, she licked my cheek. I gathered all my energy to tell her to eat me.

'Eat me, Mélodie! Eat me! Go on, what are you waiting for? Eat me. Go on, quickly!'

I shouted and screamed in vain; as soon as the words had come out of my mouth they vanished as if sucked into a hole without leaving any trace of sound. The dead man's voice wasn't reaching the ears of the dog. She then flopped down lethargically. She lay down outstretched, not wanting to get up again. A few moments later she closed her eyes; then she turned quite grey. At the same time the outline of her body blurred little by little, like the white smoke issuing from the tall chimney of public baths.

I woke up, suffocated. I was sobbing, the tears spilling from my eyes destabilising my vision of the world before me.

This took place in a park like Philosophy Park: I was in the area where the sandpit, the slides and the swings were. Dogs, a great number of them, appeared and one after the other they began running towards me, in a state of frenzy, a little like the amusing scene in Charlie Chaplin's *A Dog's Life* (1918) in which the starving tramp desperately protects little Scraps, whose food the other dogs, starving too, like him and the tramp, try to take from him. They came galloping towards me, but they didn't seem to be asking me to feed them. They were of different breeds, but, strangely, without exception all had Mélodie's head. To each dog that threw itself upon me I shouted 'Mélodie!' But none of them responded to me, none of them stopped. They ran past me and as they overtook me they threw me a doubtful, questioning, if not indifferent, look. Then they disappeared. A blonde stranger, patting her dog, a deep-brown golden retriever, gave me a puzzled, even distrustful, look. Finally she spoke to me, 'Mélodie, is that your dog's name?'

'Yes … But she died two years ago … Well, she's living somewhere else …'

'YOU ASK THAT I FORGET YOU? FEAR NOT, MY BELOVED.'

As I replied to her I found my answer bizarre. And I saw, beneath my feet, through a kind of windowpane, a buried golden retriever. She was encased in a huge glass box as clear as crystal, like those that are suggested in some enigmatic paintings of Francis Bacon's. She wasn't moving. You'd have said that time had frozen in the box. But Mélodie's body was not completely vitrified: her hairy skull emerging from the box was exposed to the refreshing cold air that I was breathing. I could touch an exposed patch of Mélodie's still-warm fur barely larger than a circle of ten centimetres in diameter.

Mélodie was there, in front of me, as alive as she was when she was in the flower of her youth, except that she remained petrified in the deathly immobility of a statue. I saw her in close-up in luminous clarity, as if I were myself in the crystal box that enclosed her, as if I could cling to her, lose myself in her. But, in fact, I was cruelly and definitively separated from her by the clear box beneath my feet without entry or opening and that, consequently, prevented me from joining her no matter what I did.

23

TO BE CONSTANT OR TO WAVER

MY THOUGHTS HAVE again returned to Hachi who waited ten years, until his last breath, for the impossible return of his dead master. If he'd lived five years longer he would have waited another five years. If he'd lived ten years longer he would have waited another ten years. Hachi's existence was an existence removed from change, from the power of time, which wears away at everything. His attachment to Professor Ueno was never worn away.

Mélodie's attachment wasn't worn away either. It didn't lose any of its strength with the passing of time. In fact it intensified.

Morning and evening, we would go for a walk together. Our walks followed the same path, with a few possible variations that added to our enjoyment. Often it was Mélodie who chose the variation to our route. When it was fine we went at a slower pace in order to taste—in my case especially by sight and in Mélodie's unquestionably by smell—the beautiful things and the surprises that the gradual passing of the days and months held in store for us, the subtle transition from one season to another. When it started to rain we would hurry to get home and wait until it had stopped. When it snowed heavily it was a celebration. She explored every inch of the snow-filled Philosophy Park where no one dared to wander, running about gleefully in every direction. The time to leave the park was virtually fixed. When I ignored it she let me know by a warning look that was innocently reproving. Each departure was a little ceremony with a real conversation in which only the human voice could be heard; each return was also a genuine ritual that finished with a short session of brushing that she must really have enjoyed as she got herself into the right position without me having to tell her.

At home we stuck together like glue. In the morning I allowed myself another moment of ritual when, before starting her meal, Mélodie looked at me for a long time until I wished her *'bon appétit'*, her impatience a disconcerting patience suffused with tenderness. When I sat working at my computer, most of the time she dozed at my feet, as peacefully as could be, or she might be in one of her favourite spots from which she could hear music playing uninterruptedly throughout the day, the volume fluctuating, with the radio tuned to a station that specialised in opera and chamber music. Her taste was my taste. Or rather, my taste had become hers.

I would go off to work for the day promising to see her again before night started to fall. Whether the promise was kept or not, without fail I found her in the front hall, sitting on her back legs, to celebrate the happy return of her master.

Drunk with joy, she jumped up to his shoulders. She held him in her front legs until she could no longer stand on her back legs; then, in a paroxysm of ecstasy, she rolled onto her back so that he could pat her stomach, which she displayed with complete trust. Actually, I think she guessed he was home again first from the sound of the car that he was parking in the garage and then from that of his footsteps echoing on the balcony tiles, which were made of some synthetic material.

When I went to France with my family we would spend periods there of from two to four weeks, and being so far away from her I lived in a state of great impatience to see her again. And when I did see her again I was met by frenetic licking and endless demonstrative jumping, which could only be stopped by the soporific effect of the shuddering rhythm of the car.

This is how the first six or seven of my years with Mélodie passed by, interspersed with periods in which I was with her every day and others, of varying length, in which she was deprived of my continuous presence. The thing that I noticed after each return, after each temporary separation that with a very human casualness and anthropocentrism I made her endure, is that the bond between us strengthened and tightened still more; she showed me—as well as, secondarily, and no doubt through me, my wife and my daughter—an attachment that was greater and deeper every day, which meant that she came to bear my absence less and less, whatever its length. She seemed truly to suffer from my departure, my disappearance from her world.

And that is why in the end I put aside any plans for a long trip and extended absence so that I would have to leave

'YOU ASK THAT I FORGET YOU? FEAR NOT, MY BELOVED.'

Mélodie as infrequently as possible. In summer I deliberately denied myself the possibility of holidaying in France. If I went away it was only for a week or ten days at the most for reasons of work that I couldn't avoid. She was no longer a young dog that you could imagine in all her vitality, beyond the reach of the ravages of time. She was showing signs of aging, which only became more pronounced without our paying them any special attention: her teeth had lost the whiteness of her early years; her face, particularly around the eyes, was covered in lighter hair than that of her golden coat, which, seen from a distance, gave the impression that she was wearing glasses with white frames.

In short we lived, Mélodie and I—and to a lesser extent all of us in our little family—a life characterised by an admirable constancy and remarkable regularity, which were those of Mélodie's inner temporal rhythm. It was quite clear that her repetitive and circular temporality was not that of humankind, which is essentially linear, and, as well as that, more and more accelerated and fleeting in our liberal democratic societies in the advanced stage of total capitalism—time always goes too quickly, we are all conscious of it, so that we are forever using the terrible word 'already': I'm already sixty; it's already two years since Mélodie left us …

Mélodie therefore lived in a world of marvellous stability, sheltered from change, and, by that very fact, she was terrified when something unexpected happened or there was an accident. So, for example, she made unaccustomed growls of suspicion when, in Philosophy Park, she first saw an old man doing exercises in which he walked backwards, doubtless to fight against the premature aging of his body. She was like another female dog, Niki, an unforgettable character in Tibor Déry's novel, who stood there 'petrified' when for the first time she saw the miner Jegyes-Molnar, the friend of Janos Ancsa, her master, make 'his ears move, first up and down, then backwards and forwards'.

Mélodie, like Hachi, like all of her kind, whether famous or unknown, lived in an eternal present that spread out across time from the most distant past to the infinitely remote future, without a hiatus, without interruption. This was no doubt the secret of her fidelity, her constancy, her incredible ability to wait—qualities she'd been endowed with but which we humans lack, for better and for worse.

A dream: I was having a private conversation with Mélodie. On the narrow footpath of a busy Parisian street I had just crossed the path of a very beautiful woman in mourning dress who bore an extraordinary resemblance to Chiara Mastroianni—perhaps it was her. I was disturbed by the sudden apparition of this beauty before me as well as by the look she'd given me for a split second just when our bodies brushed against each other as they moved along at a regular pace in opposite directions. I returned home, in a state of fear like that of a thief who has just committed a robbery and is afraid of being pursued by the police. The apartment was suffused by the peacefulness of a graveyard (which meant that I was passing from the Parisian street to the Tokyo apartment: borders are permeable in dreams). Mélodie came to meet me.

'YOU ASK THAT I FORGET YOU? FEAR NOT, MY BELOVED.'

'What's the matter, Mélodie? You seem anxious.'

'...'

'I'm so hot! I'm perspiring ...'

'...'

I took off my sopping wet tee shirt. 'You see, it's sopping wet.'

'But you're the one who seems anxious.'

'Oh, really?'

In the next scene, I told her of my furtive encounter with the beautiful woman.

'You know what, Mélodie, I'm disturbed. You can see that I am ... You're not to tell Mum about it. I've just met a very beautiful woman, an incredibly beautiful woman ... Our eyes met for a fraction of a second ... My heart has fallen victim to her charm, I couldn't help myself ... And anyway, it's not the first time it's happened to me ...'

'...'

'You won't say anything to Michèle.'

'No.'

'You don't understand me.'

'No, I don't understand you. But you said that the idea of divorce has never occurred to you ...'

'No, it hasn't, not ever. I swear it ...'

In silence, Mélodie gave me her paws one after the other.

On waking up, I told my dream to Michèle, who was lying in my arms enjoying the last seconds after emerging from sleep. It made her laugh. At that moment Mélodie leapt up and came to give us her morning greeting ... She held out her left paw to Michèle, who took it and patted it; putting her left paw down again on the tatami, she held out to me her right paw. First I kissed it and then I shook it several times as a mark of affection.

Another day, just like those before it, was beginning.

Diary Extract 6

**Fragments that Have Slipped from
the Notebook of a Dog's Companion**

If I find Hachi's absolute fidelity so unsettling, if it continues to haunt our imagination at the very heart of Tokyo's tumultuous lives, it's because it represents the impossible. We are not like Hachi, not by a long way. But if the tale of this dog who fretted away until he died from his sad and interminable wait for his master moves me to tears, if the memories of Mélodie plunge me into a rather dangerous melancholic state, it's because there is still within me a fragment of canine sensibility, like a trace, a faint echo of a distant time when our ancestors were still not completely disconnected from the wider community of living things. Man invented literature in order to set down in it the marks left by the pain he felt at the crucial moment in which he became aware of his condition as a man—undoubtedly as a *modern man*—an awareness which came out of this fundamental schism.

Around me couples are made and unmade, bursting apart like bubbles. When I write to a friend (of either sex) to whom I haven't

DIARY EXTRACT 6

written for more than a year or two the thought crosses my mind: 'Are they still together?' Westerners have taken a long time to free themselves of the religious conception of marriage. It was only in 1974 that divorce by mutual consent became possible in France. The Revolution had instituted a divorce law that was exceptionally subversive, relying only on the individual will of the man or woman. But this arrangement was too far ahead of its time and only lasted a short while. Today men and women are free to come together and to separate as they decide without the gods and priests having anything to do with it. We have dispensed with the religious illusion of the unchangeable, the constant and the eternal ... Nothing is unchangeable. Everything is subject to change. We are in time that passes ... in a becoming perpetually subject to Time that erodes, alters and transforms ...

The Princess of Cleves (1678), disparaged by a former President of the Republic,[*] bears witness to the terror of men and women before the devastating force of Time, at the very moment when they seize the individual right to love and to act as they intend, without concern for the demands and constraints of the members of the family or lineage. Madame de Clèves, when the death of her husband finally makes possible her marriage with the man she loves, paradoxically refuses to take this path dictated by passion precisely because she does not believe in the unalterability of romantic love: 'I know that

---

[*] Nicolas Sarkozy, President of France from 2007 to 2012, created a minor furore when, in 2006, he made sarcastic comments about the appeal of the classic work by Madame de Lafayette.

'YOU ASK THAT I FORGET YOU? FEAR NOT, MY BELOVED.'

you are free', she declares, 'that I am and that things are such that the world would perhaps not have cause to censure you, nor me either, if we each made an eternal commitment to the other. But do men retain their passion in such eternal commitments?' This woman who withdrew 'into a retreat and into occupations more holy than those of the most austere convents', was, ultimately, a kind of sacrificial victim immolated on the altar of History. And from this sacrifice have emerged all the more or less ephemeral couples over generations. Today we live in a world in which a talented author (Frédéric Beigbeder) can write a novel entitled *Love Lasts Three Years*.

According to Hans Robert Jauss, in *Julie, or the New Heloise* (1761), French literature of the classical era underwent a kind of *auto-da-fé*, which was incredibly wide-reaching: Corneille, Racine, La Fontaine, La Bruyère and La Rochefoucauld do not withstand the implacable literary judgement of Rousseau. With one exception, though: *The Princess of Cleves*, which he would like to be a pair with Book IV of *Julie*. If *The Princess of Cleves* kills the passion of the heroine at its source by shutting her away in a monastic life based on repetition, *Julie, or the New Heloise* does the same—hence the exceptional treatment given to the novel of Madame de Lafayette—by preventing the passionate relationship between Saint-Preux and Julie from coming to fruition, and conversely by attempting to realise the happiness of the woman in a durable and permanent state—like that of the retreat of Madame de Clèves—that marriage to the wise and impassive Wolmar guarantees. The terror of men and women before natural law, according to which everything is worn away, has also left a remarkable imprint on this work. 'There is no passion', Rousseau declares,

> that creates such a strong illusion in us as love: we take its
> violence as a sign of its lasting; the heart that is laden with such

DIARY EXTRACT 6

sweet feeling extends it so to speak into the future, and as long as this love lasts we believe that it will not come to an end. But, on the contrary, it is its very ardour that consumes it; it becomes worn away with youth; it is effaced with beauty, it is extinguished beneath the icy wastes of age; and since the world began two white-haired lovers sighing for each other is a sight that has never been seen.

Don Juan is the unfaithful one *par excellence*. Mélodie remains in an eternal present, which occupies, from the past to the future, the whole duration of time. But Don Juan lives in a temporality radically opposed to Mélodie's: he lives in a present disconnected from both the past and the future. The donjuanesque existence is that of the seducer who, thumbing his nose at the authority of the past and the promise of the future, gives himself up wholly to the exclusive pleasure of the present. It is a discontinuous existence, made up of fleeting moments of sensual delight. At the end of Molière's play (1665)—or Mozart's opera (1787)—Don Juan—or Don Giovanni—is punished by divine power represented by the statue of the Commander: he is struck down and swallowed up into the dark abyss. In the direct contrast between the discontinuity of unstable desire and the permanence of the divine order, between the fleeting present of carnal pleasure and the untouchable immobility of the dinner guest of stone, between the empty volubility of the dissolute son and the sacred word of the inflexible Father, between the modern and the ancient, it is the ancient who ultimately annihilates the modern by a radical condemnation. But it is precisely this radical condemnation, in some way fully purged, that we moderns have put aside, without shame or embarrassment, under the new guise of a super seducer addicted to the maximum intensity of moments with no tomorrow. The damnation of Don Juan,

'YOU ASK THAT I FORGET YOU? FEAR NOT, MY BELOVED.'

in the same way no doubt as Madame de Clèves in her monastic life of exemplary austerity, paved the way for the birth of all the Don Juans in the centuries to come.

Diderot, in the *Supplement to the Voyage of Bougainville* (1774), gives the Tahitian Orou the audacity to expose the absurd and untenable nature of the principles of the chaplain, his interlocutor, in the face of the 'general law of beings':

> Is there anything, in fact, that appears more unreasonable to you than a precept that proscribes the change which is in us, that demands a constancy that cannot be there and which violates the nature and freedom of the male and the female by chaining them to each other forever; than a fidelity that limits the most capricious of pleasures to the same individual; than an oath of immutability of two beings of the flesh, under a sky that is not for an instant the same, below caves that threaten ruin, at the bottom of a cliff that crumbles away, at the foot of a tree that cracks, on a stone that moves beneath you?

Unquestionably, essential to Diderot's dynamic materialism is the theme of change in all its forms, notably that of the weather that changes. We meet it throughout his work: *Rameau's Nephew*, for example, is placed 'under the malign influence of each and every Vertumnus'. Vertumnus was the god who presides over the changes of weather and season.

It is this same theme of change as the general law of beings that we meet fully developed in Mozart's *Così fan tutte* (1790).

DIARY EXTRACT 6

The plot of the *dramma giocoso* revolves around the old and lucid philosopher, Don Alfonso, who tries to disillusion the two young officers, Guglielmo and Ferrando, sad and pitiful prisoners of a stubborn illusion: the unconditional fidelity of their respective fiancées, Fiordiligi and Dorabella, the two sisters who do not for a second doubt the constancy of their own hearts. They first resist the seduction practised by their lovers, who are transformed in their disguise as Albanians, but they soon succumb. Mozart has placed towards the middle of Act One (Scene 6) a trio of sublime beauty '*Soave sia il vento* ...', sung by Fiordiligi, Dorabella and Don Alfonso just as they are saying their adieus to the two officers who are leaving their sweethearts: 'May the wind be gentle, may the waves be calm, and may all the elements, peaceful now, be responsive to our desires.' This is one of the most beautiful musical moments of the work. The music, of great serenity, marks the end of an idyllic temporality based on the permanence of things and feelings. After this moment of rupture the lovers will find themselves irremediably caught up in a process, a becoming that is fatally subject to change, to alteration, to wearing away ...

In his only opera, *Fidelio* (definitive version 1814), Beethoven celebrates the triumph of an exemplary conjugal fidelity over the political oppression of a tyrant. It is said that he had a deep aversion to *Così fan tutte* and *Don Giovanni*. That is understandable. But how is it that the music of infidelity appears to me infinitely more satisfying and complete than that of fidelity?

24

THE FINAL DAYS

ON 6 AUGUST 2009—I remember it very well because it was the day after my birthday—Michèle had left for her native land to see her elderly mother, with whom she hoped to spend most of her holidays. As for Julia-Madoka, she'd left on 18 August to go to university in Paris. So I was on my own in Tokyo with Mélodie. I was busy correcting the final proofs of the translation of *School Blues* by Daniel Pennac.

On 26 August, returning home around 4pm, I found Mélodie lying down listlessly in the kitchen near her bowl, and I'd never seen her lying there like that before.

I'd left the house at the beginning of the afternoon, around 2pm, to go and see the publisher of *School Blues*. The purpose of this brief meeting in a jazz cafe not far from Nakano Station was to hand over to her the final proof, which I'd now corrected. I stayed on a little while—the editor and I not denying ourselves the pleasure of taking the conversation beyond the strictly professional to discuss music, our common passion, and the CDs and concerts that we'd particularly enjoyed. With a somewhat unwonted enthusiasm on my part I'd talked to her in some detail about the performance of Mahler's *Fourth Symphony* conducted by Claudio Abbado that I'd listened to a few days before over the internet, live from the Festival of Lucerne. The emotion that had gripped me as I listened was extraordinarily profound; its power was unsettling; I had never experienced it before. And in fact that emotion remains unchanged: it comes back to me; I am seized by it again every time I listen to the recording of that concert. That first listening had marked the beginning of my growing interest in all of the Italian maestro's Lucerne recordings of Mahler. What is it that makes a miracle like that possible?

During our conversation, however, my thoughts kept returning to the one who was waiting for me with her patiently controlled impatience. I apologised, without giving the reason, for having to put a rather abrupt end to the conversation. I took my leave of the publisher. I got my bicycle and hurried home. When I arrived, a little breathless, it was past 4pm. It was still hot outside.

Mélodie was not in the hall. I was expecting to find her as usual behind the door and to be greeted by the full gamut of expressions signifying her uncontained joy now that the wait she'd endured was over. But no. She hadn't come to meet me. I called her. No answer. I took off my summer jacket and put my things down in my study. She wasn't in there. I kept on calling her. Silence. Panicking a little, I went into the dining room and glanced towards the kitchen. And there I saw her: she was lying down, near her bowl, she seemed exhausted, all her strength gone …

'YOU ASK THAT I FORGET YOU? FEAR NOT, MY BELOVED.'

'What's the matter, Mélodie? What's going on? Are you ill? Is something hurting?'

Mélodie didn't move. Lying on her side, fully stretched out, the look she gave me can only be described as distraught. I didn't delay before calling Mr D, the vet. The phone rang for a long time. There was no answer. I called a woman vet we'd once taken Mélodie to see when she had some mysterious problems with vomiting. At the time she'd been incompetent, but it was the closest clinic. So I resorted to ringing her. Stammering, I described Mélodie's state to her and asked her if she could come and see her. She said she couldn't because she had too many appointments. My only option was to take Mélodie by car to a third vet whose practice was a little further away. First, in the dining room, I spread out a big navy blue *furoshiki*, a square of material a metre in width that in the past we used as what I'd describe as a makeshift clothes bag. My plan was to place Mélodie on the cloth in her outstretched position, then to carry her as if in a bassinet with the help of Mrs O, a neighbour I would get to come and help me. I spoke to Mélodie, 'Mélodie, can you get up? Can you come and lie down here? We're going to see Mr K.'

She didn't move a muscle. So I picked up in my arms this body weighing about thirty kilos. Given the state of my back this was most ill-advised, but I couldn't do anything else. She gave a little groan but she didn't resist. Just when I was about to put her on the *furoshiki*, to my utter amazement she got up and stood firmly on her four feet.

'Ah, good on you ... You'll walk to the car? We'll take the lift to go down, OK? Wait, I'm going to get my things ... and your bag too ...'

The vet informed me that Mélodie's lungs were full of fluid and that it was necessary to drain it off in order to examine whether or not it showed any malignancy. I asked him to do everything necessary for her to get better again as quickly as possible.

Mélodie's condition didn't really improve. There were ups and downs in September and October. But the moments of relief became fewer and further between and gave way to those of increasingly frequent and prolonged anxiety. Mr K, his attitude one of depressing uncertainty, acknowledged his powerlessness and advised us to try to get in at one of the biggest veterinary hospitals in Tokyo, further away again and more expensive.

Finally, a large, probably cancerous, tumour was discovered above the heart. Would she have an operation? No, what good would it do? There was no point in battling an illness when it was impossible to stop its inexorable, implacable, merciless progress. That being the case I could think of one thing and one thing only, an obsession: to take any measures clinically possible and financially within our means if not to inhibit at least to lessen the dog's suffering. She was given painkilling medication and we returned home. It was 16 October 2009. Mélodie had forty-seven days ahead of her.

She was finding it more and more difficult to walk and to relieve herself. When she squatted the muscles of her back legs could no longer support her: they gave way and she made a mess. We tried to find a solution and came up with a sort of jacket with two sleeves so that we could help her to support herself.

The tumour grew bigger. It now formed a lump above her shoulder. Her legs, especially her front ones, had grown fat and round like little tree trunks. Was this because they were filling with liquid from the tumour? I don't know. She walked painfully and with difficulty, and no doubt the pain was more and more unbearable despite the medication.

Even so she kept up her morning and evening walk. Michèle and I tried to be together as often as possible in accompanying her, while the walk, which really hadn't been a walk at all for some time now, became shorter each day. In the end it had just become a matter of going out so that she could relieve herself.

A wolf howl—short, strident, desperate—shattered the silence and dragged me brutally from sleep. I gave a start and sat up. I rubbed my eyes. In the semi-darkness I saw Mélodie's head, slightly tilted to the side; she was anxious, watching me. She was lying as usual on the bath towel placed at the foot of our big bed. Michèle, who'd been in a light sleep beside me, asked what was going on.

'It's Mélodie, she's woken me up. Didn't you hear her?'

The dog repeated her howling, longer and deeper this time, pointing if not to actual pain that she was experiencing, at least to the fact that the level of discomfort was increasing. Mélodie's plaintive cry was so eloquent, so expressive, that it sounded to me like a plea for help. I went to her, she all the while continuing to watch me. The fading light from outside, wan and colourless, which was coming through the chink in the shutter, which had been left slightly open, fell on the upper half of her head, showing up her advanced years. And it accentuated the devastating power of the illness she now carried inside her. I noticed that she was panting, when hardly a few minutes before I thought that she'd been resting peacefully in the gentle warmth of the night.

'What's the matter, Mélodie? Are you in pain? Are you trying to tell me something?'

I took Mélodie's right paw, which she held out gingerly. I rubbed my cheek against hers. Then I whispered in her ear,

'You can come and lie next to me, OK?'

As soon as I'd said these words, with one movement I shifted the dog about two metres by pulling the bath towel on which she lay motionless, her intense gaze still trained on me. She was now very close to me, just ten centimetres from the edge of the bed, like a frightened child who nestles into its father's arms.

'Good night. Sleep well, *Mélodie-chan*.'

Mélodie stretched out. I placed my hand on her swollen shoulder. Then I slid it gently right down her back in the direction her fur grew. I repeated this several times. After that she became calm again, and her breathing grew regular. All the fear, all the restless anxiety of the lonely and interminable night seemed to have gone; she now abandoned herself to the powerfully reassuring and soothing feeling of not being alone, to the sensation that was at once tactile and olfactory of the immediate proximity of her human companion.

'YOU ASK THAT I FORGET YOU? FEAR NOT, MY BELOVED.'

Finally, I went to sleep, my right hand placed very lightly on her neck, its protruding lump like the sign of an unassailable morbidity.

The next morning when I woke up I found myself in exactly the same position. My hand hadn't left Mélodie's body, which was relaxed and yet very ill. She hadn't moved an inch either.

It was Wednesday, 2 December 2009. Michèle and I had to hurry because we both had an early morning start.

'Come on, *Mélodie-chan*, we're going for a little walk', said Michèle in her clear voice.

I helped to get her up. I slipped her two-sleeved jacket over her back. She began to walk, slowly, putting one foot in front of another, hesitant and uncertain. Really she was just staggering along. I remembered my father, who, in the last days of his life, wasn't very clear about the order in which to put his clothes on. After a few tottering steps Mélodie couldn't hold on any longer: she peed, just a little, in the hall. This was the first time she'd had a problem with incontinence if we don't count the accidents that occurred when her joyful outbursts got the better of her.

She started walking again. While Michèle cleaned the yellow liquid from the tiles, I went with Mélodie towards the lift, which we'd been using for several weeks now to go down to the ground floor from the first floor. Once in the street, contrary to her usual habit of waiting for her mistress, she started off straight away. She went thirty metres and stopped on the edge of the footpath on Nakano Avenue. Then she passed all the remaining urine into the gutter. She looked at me, tilting her head imperceptibly to the side in the way she had. It was a look of pleading. I understood that she couldn't or wouldn't go any further.

'I understand, Mélodie. We'll go home, we'll take it very easy.'

I took two or three steps. But Mélodie didn't follow me. 'So we're not going home?'

Mélodie threw me a second pleading look, one of infinite, heart-wrenching sadness.

She was completely exhausted. She couldn't go any further.

I picked up her body which, having given up completely, seemed heavier than when I'd had to lift it two months before when I took her to Mr K, the vet. With Mélodie in my arms I walked with quick, jerky steps. Without meaning to I pressed against the bulging area on her shoulder. She cried out as if she'd felt a surge of sharp pain. Michèle came to meet us.

'She can't walk any more, poor thing. Well, she's in a lot of pain ... I'm trying not to touch the lump but it's still hurting her ...'

I reached the house at last. She groaned with every step I took, but she calmed down completely as soon as I put her on her four feet in the little lift that took us up to the apartment. We had to hurry. I rapidly swallowed a piece of bread and butter and set to preparing Mélodie's bowl of food. To the usual kibble I added some slices of beef, some *natto* (she loved these fermented soya beans) and some boiled cabbage to stimulate her appetite. I put the meal, more elaborate than

'YOU ASK THAT I FORGET YOU? FEAR NOT, MY BELOVED.'

usual, down in front of her, now she'd gone to lie down on the bath towel at the foot of the bed of her master and mistress. She didn't get up; she showed no interest in what I'd given her. For the first time she didn't want to touch her food. I put a little bit of cabbage and *natto* on the palm of my left hand and put it under her lips. To no avail, she wasn't interested. I wanted to look at her tongue; I was struck by the pale colour of her gums, which had always looked bright pink to me in contrast to the yellowish white colour of her teeth.

'You don't want to eat? It's good, really it is.'

'...'

'You aren't well. I know. I have to leave you, I'm afraid. I'll come back as soon as I can, when I'm finished. You'll wait for me. OK?'

'...'

'Michèle has to go too. But she'll be back soon, before me. You'll be on your own, but don't worry. It'll be all right. You'll look after the house for us, won't you?'

I didn't know what to say. The day, its every second waiting to crush me beneath its great burden of worry, was beginning.

Michèle, now ready to leave, said goodbye to her in turn. Mélodie watched us moving away from her, impassively. I picked up my briefcase, and we went out. We kissed each other in front of the house and went our separate ways. Michèle went down the street to the subway, I took my bicycle.

When I reached the end of the street that runs into Nakano Avenue I stopped for a moment. My eyes turned towards the edge of the still-wet footpath. I wanted to retrace my steps. I went back. I opened the front gate, I went up the stairs, I put the key in the lock. Mélodie wasn't in the hall. In fact she hadn't budged. She was on her bath towel, her muzzle on her swollen legs the size of two little tree trunks.

'It's me again, *Mélodie-chan* … I came back to tell you to have a good day. I don't think I said that to you just now … I'll see you this evening.'

I rubbed my cheek against hers, the right and the left. I could feel that they were colder than usual.

25

CREMATION

MÉLODIE LEFT US on 2 December 2009 at 5.37pm. It had begun to rain in the afternoon, and the rain, accompanied at times by a howling wind, kept falling until dawn.

She'd spent the whole day without moving, or changing her position. All she did was wait for the return of her master and mistress, in an aching, drowsy impatience. The wait wasn't over for her until Michèle, first of all, had come back to her around three o'clock. She had rushed home when her work was finished, and Mélodie licked the hand that her mistress held out to her. Michèle stroked her head. Mélodie seemed to give in completely, with no resistance, to the sleepiness that was flooding over her.

Close to five o'clock, Michèle, busy at the other end of the apartment, went to see Mélodie. Much to her surprise, Mélodie had shifted position. She was no longer on the big bath towel at the foot of our bed. She'd gone back to the spot

I'd made for her the previous night after her lacerating howls, settling just next to my side of the big marital bed. With her eyes closed, she put her tired muzzle on the edge of the bed as if she were breathing in all the smells of my body that impregnated the bedclothes.

The rain became heavier; the wind blew wildly. Michèle was afraid that the bad weather would turn into a real storm. She wanted to go to the closest shop and get a few things that she needed to prepare the dinner. She put on her yellow rain hat and opened the wardrobe to get her coat, putting it on as she went to the kitchen to turn off the gas, a habit she'd gotten into through living here for many years, in a country subject to violent earthquakes.

Mélodie heard the sound of the wardrobe opening and closing. She made an incredible effort to get up and, especially, to move from where she was so that she could see her mistress, who was getting ready to brave the wind and the rain. When she planted herself in the living room in front of Michèle, who was coming back from the kitchen, she was out of breath. She collapsed, throwing a despairing glance at the one who was going to abandon her for a time.

'Oh, good heavens, you've got up, *Mélodie-chan*? I was coming to see you and tell you that I was going out to do some shopping …'

'…'

'I'll come straight back.'

'…'

'YOU ASK THAT I FORGET YOU? FEAR NOT, MY BELOVED.'

Looking up at her, Mélodie's eyes, candid and intense at the same time, clear, moist and utterly beseeching, pierced Michèle's heart. She'd got the message at once. Everything in this infinitely weak and weakened being, vulnerable and made vulnerable like an abandoned child, everything about her, from the superhuman effort to get up, to her gaze brimming with tenderness and fear, said to her: 'Stay, please. Don't go.'

With her coat and hat still on, Michèle knelt down beside the dog. Mélodie stretched out fully, then gave a first death cry. Then, a few seconds later, a second one.

A heavy silence fell.

'No, Mélodie, please …'

Finally, the body of the dog stiffened convulsively in the last death throes. That was all.

On Sunday, 6 December, I had to conduct an in-conversation session with my film director friend Malek Bensmaïl about the film *China Is Still Far Away* that he'd just made. On Thursday, 3 December, in the afternoon, I had a meeting with the technical team for the event to familiarise myself with the venue and the electronic set-up for the projection of the sequences I'd chosen in agreement with Malek. So all in all the end of the week was looking very full. For this being, this dog, this animal who'd just died and who'd been with us for twelve years, we promised ourselves long days of mourning and remembrance; for this life that was moving into the distance we needed an intense time of prayer, away from anthropocentric religions and denominational allegiance. Michèle and I had therefore decided to have Mélodie's cremation the day after the event of 6 December.

CREMATION

Until then, for four whole days, we had to preserve Mélodie's body and slow down the process of decomposition and putrefaction. For this purpose we bought up bags of ice blocks in considerable amounts. In four days we had gone through the stocks of the supermarkets in our neighbourhood. A young man at the till smiled and said to me, 'You're often having parties, I'm envious!'

'No, no, there's nothing to be envious about. It's no joke, I can tell you …'

Mélodie's body had been placed in the dining room, on her mattress, which in the end she only lay on from time to time during the day. It was surrounded by some dozens of bags of ice and a number of bunches of brightly coloured flowers that Michèle had herself carefully chosen from her florist. To conceal the very commercialised ugliness of the ice bags covered in advertising we'd used navy blue *furoshiki* with floral patterns, which created a striking contrast with the red of the anemones and the orangey yellow of the carnations. On a thin Japanese cushion (*zabuton*), Michèle had collected together all the toys and objects recalling the departed animal's presence among us. A little candle in a candleholder in the style of an old-fashioned European lamp sparkled in the semi-darkness. It was a tomb. A true tomb.

The four days passed slowly. Each evening, following the numbing hours spent with humans, we resumed our moments of secret intimacy in the company of the inanimate body of the dog. The presence of the dead animal may not have taken

'YOU ASK THAT I FORGET YOU? FEAR NOT, MY BELOVED.'

away the fatigue of the day but at least it allowed us to forget it for a time.

On the morning of Monday, 7 December, we went to the crematorium attached to a Buddhist temple next to Philosophy Park. Thanks to a big billboard that I looked at without paying it any particular attention, I knew that there was a cemetery for pets on the other side of the wall that looks down over Shin-Ome Avenue. When I was out walking with Mélodie, there'd been a few times that I'd said to myself that we might go there one day, but this barely hinted-at possibility was pushed back down again into the dark and hidden corners of my mind. But that morning that was precisely where we were going ...

I had arranged and settled everything for the manner and conduct of Mélodie's cremation in a phone call I'd had with a woman who was an employee of the crematorium. There was to be no reading from some sacred text by an ecclesiastic. No religious ceremony. No pointlessly luxurious casket that only serves to make a temple that is already wealthy wealthier still. I especially didn't want to be part of the buying and selling of sacred posthumous names: I therefore politely declined the purchase of a mortuary plaque with a Buddhist name engraved on it, something that had been suggested as if it were for a human being. In all of this I remained faithful to my father, who, anticipating old age, had so often repeated to me: 'No monks—above all, no monks—when I die. Do you hear me? Everything comes down to the market and everything is marketable, even death ... I don't agree with it ...' The repulsion my father felt in relation to Buddhist priests and which he didn't hide—I return to it again—was very much in my mind. Mélodie's death didn't cost us a lot: a small sum covering the cremation expenses, a bunch of flowers and a quarter of an hour of reflection in a tiny chapel that we'd wanted to give ourselves in the presence of Mélodie's now completely stiff, cold body, just before it was reduced to smoke and ashes.

We had laid Mélodie out on a big *furoshiki*. This enabled us to carry her easily and to put her down slowly and carefully as if she were lying on a stretcher. I noticed that her tongue had escaped slightly from her mouth, its involuntary distension frozen. I felt that death inhabited her body now, once and for all. When we got to the garage we placed her in the boot of the car, which I'd cleaned in readiness.

Five minutes later we were at the crematorium. A young woman dressed in black was waiting for us. I opened the boot of the car. Two men in funeral dress came forward and bowed to the remains of Mélodie, laid out on the *furoshiki*. Then they put her into a coffin of reinforced cardboard. The young woman in black said a few words to us about what was to follow, while the coffin moved away from us in the direction of a little pavilion by the cemetery. She first showed us into the front office to give us some paperwork about the cremation; then without hurrying she took us to the little pavilion, the chapel where we were invited to say our goodbyes to Mélodie in the presence of her inanimate body, which we were looking at for the last time.

We entered the little chapel. The cardboard coffin was already placed on the altar. Just next to Mélodie's head Michèle put the bunch of anemones and carnations that had kept her company over the past four days. She added

'YOU ASK THAT I FORGET YOU? FEAR NOT, MY BELOVED.'

to it two single flowers, pure white, which she'd picked from our garden a few minutes before we left that morning. Beside the coffin there was a pedestal table on which were placed a lighted candle, an incense holder with three sticks of burning incense, a brass bell in the shape of a cup that is rung once or twice with a little stick to begin the prayer and, finally, an identification label for the animal. It read: 'Mélodie Mizubayashi deceased 2 December 2009'. I noticed that Mélodie's name was placed conspicuously next to that of Mizubayashi. It was the first—and last—time that our dog was called *Mélodie Mizubayashi*. This joining together of the two names, unexpected but in fact completely normal, unsettled me: it made me aware of the fact that Mélodie had never existed, in reality, except as a *thing* named Mélodie, and that as such nothing distinguished her, for example, from a soft toy, a little monkey, to which Julia-Madoka, as a school girl, had given the name Zephyr. I am a human animal, a living being and a human being, and, as a result, legally speaking, I am part of the category of persons as they are defined in the Civil Code. But in Mélodie's case, she is a non-human animal, a living being but not human. And this status of 'non-human' is decisive and is sufficient for her to be considered as a thing even though she lives, or an asset belonging to a person even though, endowed with life, she is, quite clearly, more than a simply material asset. Mélodie, in fact, has never had the place she deserves in our world, which is built on the exclusive dichotomy of Persons and Things. A great philosopher once said, 'Animals perish, man dies'. Does this mean that Mélodie was merely a perishable thing? And did she in fact perish? I cannot think so.

In this respect one thing is perhaps worth noting. There are languages, like Japanese, which still have echoes, however weak they may be, of a distant time in which men, still having no conception of a Civil Code, living in proximity with animals, thought that they formed one and the same community with them. Thus while French reserves for humans the use of nouns like face, mouth, nose, foot and the verb for giving birth, for example, Japanese uses these terms for humans and beasts alike without marking any clear dividing line between them. As for the word for beast, which signals that the speaker of French, in using it, can only be associating the animal with stupidity, I won't hide my reluctance to use it. Having said that, I must admit that I'm uneasy about the Japanese word for stupid, *baka*, which is written with two ideograms meaning horse and deer. But let me return to Mélodie.

We remained in front of the coffin for a good quarter of an hour. We prayed. I put my hands together and closed my eyes as I do, on occasion, at the grave of my father at the Kodaira Cemetery as well as at my mother's house, before the family altar in which memory of the ancestors is preserved by means of a number of miniature steles erected in their honour. I had never felt this need to pray as intensely since the passing of my father. A man without faith, without religion, I don't know if the word *pray* is appropriate to the sudden eruption of this inner call that filled me with emotion, that obliged me to prostrate myself before the inert body of the animal, an inner call that prompted me to gather up inside me the whole of my attention, the whole of my energy of remembering to merge with the flow of images that would soon replace the quite extraordinarily intense presence of the beloved being.

'YOU ASK THAT I FORGET YOU? FEAR NOT, MY BELOVED.'

I looked at Mélodie's eyes. They no longer looked at me, they no longer spoke to me; her soul had departed somewhere through these weakly open windows. I pressed my cheek against hers—it was icy cold—for the last time. Michèle did the same. We couldn't bring ourselves to turn and go. But we had to. I signalled to the young woman in black. We left the chapel, death in our soul.

We had to wait several hours for the cremation to be completed. We waited at home for the call from the crematorium. Towards five o'clock the telephone rang. It was over ... We went to pick up Mélodie's ashes. We were given a big box containing the urn. It was a silver-coated box just like that used for a human being.

I opened the box; I removed the lid of the urn. I saw the skull almost intact and some large pieces of bone: ribs, vertebrae, tibias. At the bottom there were bones that were now just crumbs and powder.

So Mélodie had once and for all entered the kingdom of the dead. I was utterly crushed and ground down beneath an unbearable, nameless block of sadness bearing down on me. I had fallen to the bottom of an abyss of infinite dejection with no hope of being able to climb out of it again. More than anything else, I was obsessed by the thought that I hadn't been able to be at her side and to take her in my arms just as she breathed her last. I couldn't get over it, just as I'd never been able to get over the fact that I hadn't been at my dying father's side fifteen years before. I couldn't get over having missed the very last meeting, of having been deprived of the chance to thank her for all the good things she'd given me.

CREMATION

I would have recited love poems to her, flooded her ears with bewitching music. The one consolation was to know that she had passed away under Michèle's infinitely tender, kind and compassionate gaze.

What did you see, my friend, in the last moments of your life, just before passing to the other side of that line? What are the images that were projected onto the screen of your heavy eyelids? What were the moments of your existence that came back to you at the very instant you were about to pass into the other world? For I believe in your existence. Having lived so intensely in your company I know that you had a true, individual, singular and irreducible existence made up of moments differentiated according to the feeling of well-being, or its opposite, that you experienced throughout your life. One day, do you remember, in an imaginary conversation I had with you, I asked myself the same questions about my father who passed away in the nocturnal solitude of a modest Tokyo hospital. Of course, these questions will never be answered. No one, not my father, nor you, nor any other being whether human or animal, can give us their answer about what they saw during their fall into nothingness. But the unfortunate living will always ask these questions; they'll ask them of themselves, ceaselessly, tirelessly, because it is the very uncertainty and unknowability of these questions—the whole imaginary space that they discreetly allow to be opened up—that, undoubtedly, attaches the living to the dead whose memory they need to perpetuate if they are to continue to live. All that I know, or rather all that I can imagine of the last moments of your existence and that of my father,

'YOU ASK THAT I FORGET YOU? FEAR NOT, MY BELOVED.'

is the progressive diminution of consciousness, the erasure of the visible, the audible gradually fading to extinction, the dark shadows flooding in, the loss of all things, then finally nothingness ... Who could come up with a more fitting, more profound and more moving expression of this than in the last bars of the final movement, the stunning 'Adagio, Very Slow and Restrained' of Gustav Mahler's *Ninth Symphony in D Major*, the last of the symphonies if we leave aside the *Tenth*, which remained unfinished?

I rediscovered this music eight months after Mélodie's passing. Claudio Abbado performed it at the Festival of Lucerne on 19, 20 and 21 August 2010. He had enthralled me, as I've said, with Mahler's *Fourth*, which he had conducted the previous year in Lucerne. A few days later I was able to listen to the live recording of one of these concerts over the internet (I thank God for the internet). It was an epiphany, an illumination, a revelation. At the end of the work, whose performance lasted more than eighty minutes, the notes stretched out, gradually dying away until finally they had become nothing more than a kind of breath, an exhalation, barely audible. The last four notes played *pianissimo* by the violas, following the composer's notation—'*ersterbend* (dying away)', literally destroying themselves. Slowly, very slowly, the music gave way to silence, a silence that lasted more than two minutes, like a prayer for eternal life, and there was not a breath or the merest stifled cough that dared disturb it ... The tears kept flowing down my cheeks. At the edge of my consciousness there appeared two faces: Mélodie's and my father's, superimposed ...

More than two years after Mélodie's death, the silver box containing her urn is still in the same place, as if it couldn't be uprooted, as if I'd erected her tomb in the dining room just where her mattress bed used to be. I haven't dared and still do not dare to ask my mother to take Mélodie's remains into the vault of the family grave at Kodaira, just beside those of my father. I'm afraid of what she'll say. But I tell myself at the same time that Mélodie will be better off here, in this apartment, our apartment, or in our tiny garden, next to the vigorous quince tree Michèle planted a long time ago now. She lived here, she died here. She will remain here.

Mélodie, my friend, I shall not forget you. How could I forget you? How could I possibly forget you? Suddenly a concert aria by Mozart for soprano, piano and orchestra comes back to me. It is 'You ask that I forget you? Fear not, my beloved.' It is the one he composed in 1786 for Nancy Storace, the creator of the marvellous role of Suzanne in *The Marriage of Figaro* performed on 1 May 1786, in Vienna. This aria was performed, they say, during a farewell concert for her in Vienna on 27 February 1787. It was of course Mozart who accompanied her on the piano. He loved Nancy Storace. The music says so. If I could play the piano, and if I'd been

'YOU ASK THAT I FORGET YOU? FEAR NOT, MY BELOVED.'

with you just at the moment this odious cancer bore you away, I would perhaps have had the mad, extravagant idea of getting you to listen to even just the few bars, infinitely tender, where the piano enters the *rondo*. To know that you were accompanied in your walk towards death by this wonderfully gentle piece of music would have helped me to bear the unbearable.

I shall long keep in my personal box of treasures your name, and all the images, and all the music that it awakens in me.

26

MÉLODIE AND HER COMPANION

MÉLODIE OCCUPIES A considerable place in the life of her walking companion. It isn't because she lived with him and close by him for a little more than twelve years. Is twelve years of life shared a short time or a long one? That depends. But here the actual duration is not really a consideration. If the dog occupies a considerable place in the life of her companion, it is because, after having accompanied her throughout her existence, he feels that he learnt something important from her, that he received lessons from her that make the life he leads even just a little better, a little more worthy, more self-aware in any case than if he hadn't known her.

To live with Mélodie was for him, more than anything, the chance to learn to step back, somehow to separate himself from himself, to see himself as a complete stranger, to strip himself, in his imagination, of everything that made him exist as a man living in society with all that that entailed in terms of practices, habits, expected forms of behaviour, in short of what perhaps sociologists call the *habitus*.

The relationship that his dog had with him was based solely—does this need to be said?—on what he was outside all the social attributes that were ascribed to him, all the social garments that he wore selectively in life's different situations. We can invoke once again the Rousseauian image of the social man compared to that of Glaucus, the divine statue disfigured by 'time, the sea and storms'. The author of the *Second Discourse* wrote in 1755,

> ... the human soul altered in society by a thousand causes ceaselessly reborn, by the acquisition of a mass of learning and a multitude of errors, by the changes that have come about in bodily constitution, and by the continual shock of the passions has, so to speak, changed its appearance to the point of being almost unrecognisable; and all that one now finds there, instead of a being acting always according to sure and unchanging principles, instead of this celestial and majestic simplicity that its creator had stamped upon it, is, in unnatural contrast, passion which thinks it can reason and understanding in a state of delirium.

Mélodie, by her animal constitution, was only able to see in her companion his naked self, stripped of all external attributes. In the presence of a dog who was not naked because she was naked, he had become naked because, without being naked, he had the feeling that he existed in his nakedness. Like Argus, the dog of Ulysses, King of Ithaca, who, after twenty years of being apart from him, recognises his master despite him looking like an old beggar, or like Rainbow, the little dog of Joe Wilson (played by Spencer Tracy) in Fritz Lang's *Fury* (1936), who throws himself into the arms of his master who has been unjustly imprisoned and is the victim of an arson attack by a crazed lynch mob, Mélodie demonstrated her affection to her walking companion, an affection that was based on nothing external to the affection he felt towards her and to the attention he constantly paid her. The fact that he was an ordinary man now on the threshold of old age and worried about halting his incipient baldness, that he was a university lecturer, that he was the author of several books, that he was sufficiently comfortable to have quite a big house in Tokyo and so on, Mélodie was clearly supremely indifferent to all of this. Is there any human being alive capable of detaching themselves to this extent from the social situation occupied by the person with whom they are conversing?

A memory comes back to me.

A young man had just been appointed to a lectureship in a private university in Tokyo. One day he needed to check a couple more details in a rather rare book held only in the library of another university at which, in fact, he'd done his Masters and doctorate. And so, armed with a letter of recommendation from the university at which he worked, he presented himself to the Arts Faculty office in his original university, which was to provide him with a reader's card for the library. For this he had to see a clerical officer of about thirty. Doubtless Mélodie's walking companion still looked like an older undergraduate or a young PhD student: the clerk treated him with technocratic arrogance. The young lecturer

'YOU ASK THAT I FORGET YOU? FEAR NOT, MY BELOVED.'

was particularly shocked by the haughty manner in which he had almost flung him a student card to fill in. He pointed out that he was no longer a student at this establishment, but that he was now teaching at the University of M. A look of amazement and embarrassment came across the clerk's face; his manner changed completely. After that things proceeded quickly. Comfortably sitting in a reading room reserved for teaching staff, Mélodie's lecturer-cum-future-companion was able to look at the rare book in question.

He remembers another occasion. At one time, in Tokyo, he worked for a very large Japanese import-export company, NSI, as interpreter-translator. He did not yet have a position at the university, so it was important for him to act as an interpreter as often as he could to earn himself some income. A minister of an Arab country was making a courtesy visit to the board of directors of NSI. Mélodie's walking companion was first greeted by a man who, from his big office, reigned as absolute and undisputed master over the fourth floor of an imposing building belonging to the company. He explained to the sometime interpreter that the meeting with the minister was to take place on the twentieth floor, where the office of the chairman of the company was situated. They went up in the lift. The door opened. A dozen rather elderly men, all wearing grey or navy blue suits—swaggering, acting like VIPs—were there in a kind of reception hall. A curious spectacle was then played out in front of the interpreter. The man who reigned as absolute and undisputed master on the fourth floor noticed that the shoes of one of the big directors had a little dust on them. He made his way towards his superior—someone who for him was 'above the clouds', as the saying goes in his language—rubbing his hands together as he did so. Keeping his back bent, he was like an ape and reminded me in his posture and gestures of the frightful character of the sheriff in Akira Kurosawa's extraordinary film *Yojimbo*: at the end of the film the righter of wrongs, a man not bound by any ties, tells the sheriff to disappear from the world by hanging himself. The man from the fourth floor said a few words to the big director and, crouching down, began to clean his shoes with a towelling cloth that he'd taken from his pocket. The task completed, he disappeared.

From when I was a child I've always had an aversion to those like the clerk at the university or the little director from the fourth floor. Their common denominator is this very human skill in adopting a superior attitude or, conversely, a submissive one, according to the social status of the person they happen to be with. But since meeting Mélodie this aversion has turned into horror. I have come to hate these chameleons who are flatterers with the powerful, and tyrants, if not sadists, with the weak. That is why I especially like the passage from Milan Kundera's *The Unbearable Lightness of Being* that I have used as an epigraph at the front of this book. Kundera speaks of the 'fundamental débâcle' of mankind in the context of the image of Tereza stroking the head of Karenin, her dog. Because how many men and women are there who would get a satisfactory mark if they sat for 'mankind's true moral test' as defined by the novelist? And what if the one who obtained the highest mark were Nietzsche? At the cost of

'YOU ASK THAT I FORGET YOU? FEAR NOT, MY BELOVED.'

his legendary madness, which Kundera himself refers to and comments upon in these terms:

> ... Nietzsche leaving his hotel in Turin. Seeing a horse and a coachman beating it with a whip, Nietzsche went up to the horse and, before the coachman's very eyes, put his arms around the horse's neck and burst into tears.
>
> That took place in 1889, when Nietzsche, too, had removed himself from the world of people. In other words, it was at the time when his mental illness had just erupted. But for that very reason I feel his gesture has broad implications: Nietzsche was trying to apologize to the horse for Descartes. His lunacy (that is, his final break with mankind) began at the very moment he burst into tears over the horse.

Two stray dogs that I met and loved in my Tokyo childhood stay in my memory. The first is the one I've already mentioned, the Snowy who seemed lost and helpless under a driving rain, the little dog I'd brought home with me to offer him the hospitality of a night.

The second was an abandoned white puppy that I must have found somewhere or other. I was older than I was at the time of the first episode. So I knew that the puppy would not find a refuge at my house. Then I had the idea of bringing him up in secret, with a few friends from the neighbourhood, in a bamboo grove not far from home where I played with them every day. There were three or four of us in our gang. I recall the dog's face but not those of my friends. Was my affection for the puppy stronger than the childish friendship that joined me to them? Undoubtedly.

First we built a kennel of thick cardboard so that he could shelter, more or less, from the sun, the rain and the wind. And we tied him to a shrub with a little rope long enough for him to have some freedom of movement. So, for a few weeks, we had the joy of having our dog close by and seeing him grow up more quickly than us. I didn't say anything about him to my parents, or rather to my mother, because my father didn't involve himself in such matters. I was afraid that my mother would forbid me having any part in it; that she would force me to part with the dog; that she would prevent me from giving him the previous day's rice and other leftovers, which I secreted away without her knowing. I was a bit like the young Katsushiro in *Seven Samurai*, who goes without a second bowl of rice to go and offer it to Shino, the beautiful young girl of the village who is kept hidden and with whom he is secretly in love …

But I wanted to give our puppy something other than cold rice—I don't remember the name we'd given him, or perhaps we hadn't given him a name. Was he simply called Shiro (White) from the colour of his fur?—For that I needed money. My pocket money—10 yen per day—was not enough. So what did I do? I stole. It's the only time in my entire life that I've experienced the guilt of stealing. My first and last theft was due to the love I had for a lost white puppy, a little dog without a home or support or protection. I must have stolen several times for Shiro, but all the scenes of theft merge in my mind to form just one, of which I've kept a vivid image: acting stealthily so that no one saw me, I was bold enough to open the drawer of the little kitchen cupboard with the intention of taking my mother's purse. I took from

'YOU ASK THAT I FORGET YOU? FEAR NOT, MY BELOVED.'

it several 10-yen pieces, just enough to buy milk and bread ... I don't know if my friends did the same, but my life with the white puppy carried along like this with great regularity until the day when, suddenly, he was no longer there in our beloved bamboo grove.

He had disappeared. Completely. No trace of him remained. As if he'd vanished into thin air ... A great sadness flooded over me and almost prevented me from breathing. I couldn't get over this loss. This sadness, well preserved in the depths of my emotional archives, is like the big raised scar that I have above my navel, many years after the removal of my gall bladder. It still hurts when you press on it. But the weeks went by; the months flew past ... In the end I no longer thought about my puppy.

Five or six months later, when I passed in front of a big white house with a garden looking on to the street that was fenced by a bamboo hedge in the middle of which there was an iron gate, I saw a grey-white dog that reminded me of my puppy. I stopped dead. It was him. I said to him, 'Oh! What a surprise! What a surprise to find you here! Is it you? Do you recognise me?'

'...'

'Are you happy here? Is everything all right?'

He stared at me, all the while furiously wagging his tail. At that moment someone came out the front door. I went away without being able to say a proper goodbye to my dog.

The next day I went back again. I couldn't see him. For several days I kept passing in front of the big white house. But my white puppy who'd turned into a handsome grey-white dog wasn't there again.

Maybe it was just a dream? The trace of a dream that I'd retained? Perhaps, perhaps not, but the image of that white puppy has never been erased from my memory.

Leaving aside the two dogs from my childhood, Mélodie was the weakest, the most fragile being I'd known, the being most completely reduced to a state of constant powerlessness. And through this extreme vulnerability, throughout her existence, which was interwoven with mine, she held the position of teacher and I that of pupil. She was like a grand master of a traditional Japanese art whose teaching consists of saying nothing about his art and leaving his pupil to make out its quintessence. Certainly I taught her many things, among them a number of very strict rules of behaviour with the intention, as I've already pointed out, of granting her the greatest possible freedom in the world of human beings (she was practically never tied up; except for rare occasions she was always off the leash). But once this initial period of apprenticeship had passed, as a general rule it was she who tested me, asked questions of me without being aware of it, it was she who put me on the path of morality, if we understand morality to be, as Kundera seems to suggest, empathy and compassion felt towards the powerless, if not suffering beings, the ability to protect those who are defenceless, the categorical refusal to consider them as inferior beings comparable, following the Civil Code in the case of animals, to things to be used as one chooses.

'YOU ASK THAT I FORGET YOU? FEAR NOT, MY BELOVED.'

Charlie Chaplin again comes to mind. The homeless man in *City Lights* (1931), dressed in the now-threadbare suit of a middle class man, who shows such compassion to the blind flower seller, a poverty-stricken young girl; the vagabond in *The Circus* (1928), who gives his one bit of bread and a hard-boiled egg to the beautiful horseback rider who is mistreated by the ring master; to the poor glazier in *The Kid* (1921), who takes in and raises the abandoned baby; and of course the starving tramp in *A Dog's Life* (1918), who, despite belonging to the *lumpenproletariat*, decides to keep the weakest of the dogs and plans to help the unhappy dance hall singer.

The wonderful look that Charlie gives. It's the look that, universally, those who are the most dispossessed of all cast on the creatures that are faring the worst—*creature* is the only word, I think, capable of indicating both the *being accorded the status of 'person'* and the *being not accorded the status of 'person'*: people and animals. It is, finally, the look in which morality is held secure; it would certainly not have struck me with the same intensity if I hadn't known Mélodie's—one of primal innocence and incredibly disarming strength, the same look that apprehended me, above and below the mirrored surface of every disguise and adornment, in my essential nakedness.

It is said that the dog is the only being on earth that loves you more than it loves itself. Mélodie loved me. But it is my naked self that she loved.

The second of Mélodie's great lessons, which in fact flows from the first, is, if I can put it like this, her sincerity. Mélodie was a being who never deceived—this is an unshakeable truth that I feel intimately, deep inside me. Not to deceive is to remain faithful. Faithfulness is the ability to wait indefinitely for the return of the one you love. Hachi and Argus, as we have seen, are two figures who are emblematic of absolute fidelity. And I would readily associate Mélodie with these two mythical dogs.

But to deceive is also to lie, to have recourse to more or less subtle and complex calculations to turn a situation to one's advantage. That is precisely what Mélodie didn't know how to do. That type of behaviour was quite foreign to her makeup. Did she lie to get more food or water? No. If there wasn't any more, she was happy with what she had. Or she simply waited. She waited until we put nice food in her dish or fresh water in her bowl. Did she pretend that she was ill so that she didn't have to go for a walk? No. If she didn't want to go for a walk it was because she really was ill. Mélodie didn't lie, didn't deceive, didn't get caught up in selfish calculations because her life was ordered in such a way that she had nothing to gain to the detriment of anyone else. She lived a solitary and, if I may say, minimal existence, which did no harm to others. Her existence was a small miracle because it was removed from any violence. In this respect it made me think of that of Bartleby, the scribe who seeks somehow to efface himself by replying to every question with 'I would prefer not to …' For a human being, to exist is already to exercise violence in some way. To speak, to speak out, is already sometimes to wound, at least to embark on an action that is more or less violent in relation to the world, to certain beings, no matter how small that action is … Let me take a very trivial example.

'YOU ASK THAT I FORGET YOU? FEAR NOT, MY BELOVED.'

If a married man loves a married woman who is not his wife and writes to her to declare his love to her, while admitting this extramarital love to his own wife, surely this is to exercise violence over both of the women simultaneously by sowing disorder in their peaceful lives, even if, thanks to the wisdom of each of the protagonists, nothing, finally, at least on the surface, changes the normal course of their lives! Mélodie was unaware of this primary drawback of human existence. Almost alone in the world with me and my little family, she never found herself in a situation of permanent competition or of continuous psychological warfare with others. Not made for plotting and scheming, she was supremely at peace with herself.

Diary Extract 7

Fragments that Have Slipped from the Notebook of a Dog's Companion

In his very engaging book *The Philosopher and the Wolf*, Mark Rowlands explains that a wolf and a dog, even though they can express themselves, cannot lie to us. To convince us of this he relates an amusing episode in which Brenin, the wolf who shared his life for more than a decade, plays a revealing role. The philosopher was in the middle of swallowing a 'microwaveable plate of monosodium glutamate known as a Hungry Man meal'. Brenin, lying next to him, was 'watching like a hawk'. The telephone rang in the next room. The philosopher went to answer it, leaving the food on the table. A few seconds later he returned to continue his meal while Brenin, 'having quickly devoured [the] Hungry Man meal, was making his way rapidly over to his bed on the other side of the room'. The return of the philosopher, 'unwelcome, but not entirely unexpected', nailed the wolf to the spot. He was frozen, says Rowlands, 'in mid-stride, one leg in front of the other, his face turned towards me'. He was literally petrified. The message expressed with the whole of his body was clear:

'YOU ASK THAT I FORGET YOU? FEAR NOT, MY BELOVED.'

'Busted!' It was neither 'I don't know how your plate got like that! I didn't do it. It was like that when I got here', nor 'you finished it before you left, you senile old bastard'. And the philosopher then adds: 'They [wolves] can talk. And what's more, we can understand them. What they cannot do is lie. And that is why they have no place in a civilized society. A wolf cannot lie to us; neither can a dog. That is why we think we are better than them.'

Rowlands develops the idea that in the world of living things only the ape has a way of living based on self-interest and deceit. In the course of a long history of biological evolution, as a consequence of the social way of life that it has chosen, the ape came to acquire, as well as mechanical intelligence (the ability to enter into a relationship with the natural world) shared by other animals, a social intelligence (also described as Machiavellian), which lies in the ability to deceive, to manipulate and to exploit those of its own kind. 'The ape', says the philosopher, 'is the tendency to see life as a process of gauging probabilities and computing possibilities, and using the results of these computations in its favour.' This is a particular form of intelligence corresponding to a stage of cognitive development belonging to the primates. A single example will suffice, that of a baboon that keeps for itself a vine (a favourite food of baboons) instead of sharing it with its fellow baboons. It is an example that is sadly revealing of the Machiavellian intelligence with which we are endowed:

> A troop of baboons is travelling along a narrow trail. One baboon, female S, spots a nearly obscured clump of Loranthus—a vine that is highly prized by the baboon palate—in one of the trees. Without looking at the others, S sits down at the side of the trail and begins intently self-grooming. The others pass her by and, when they are out of sight, she leaps up into the tree and eats the vine.

DIARY EXTRACT 7

The behaviour of S is no different from 'pretending you have to tie your shoelace when you have, in fact, spotted a twenty-pound note lying on the ground'. It is somewhat disconcerting to note the similarity between the baboon enjoying the delicious vine on her own and someone who wants to pocket the twenty-pound note surreptitiously. But it is even more disconcerting to know that it is in our case, with human beings, that this ability at cheating reaches its very highest point.

We are therefore, according to Rowlands, prisoners of a simian mode of existence, which results from the fact that apes, at a given moment of the general evolution of species, took a path leading to civilisation, one radically different from that of wolves.

I like *The Philosopher and the Wolf*. Many passages touch me because they resonate with the years I passed with Mélodie. But I feel the need to comment briefly on the use the author makes of this word *civilisation*.

Rowlands infers that there is a line of demarcation separating the primates from other living things and that this line of demarcation is called civilisation. On the one side a world whose structure is societal, essentially characterised by the practice of deception; on the other a world inhabited by the solitary animals unaware of this practice. Agreed. But it seems to me that the idea is enhanced by refining the concept of civilisation a little more, by introducing into the very heart of the world of living beings the opposition between civilisation and non-civilisation—what can be called, without attaching the slightest pejorative nuance to it, barbarism. In the very long history of humanity the state of barbarism precedes civilisation, which only dates from yesterday. And in the case of Western Europe the absolutist seventeenth century is, according to Norbert Elias, the moment when the civilising process is affirmed. The society of the

'YOU ASK THAT I FORGET YOU? FEAR NOT, MY BELOVED.'

court, at its apogee under Louis XIV, is a world subject to unceasing measures of self-control in hiding one's emotions on the part of all of its members. For confirmation of this we need only turn to a page of *The Misanthrope* or *The Princess of Cleves*, or to reread La Bruyère's *Characters*. Or to recall one of La Rochefoucauld's maxims, for example, 'Humility is often only a feigned submission which one employs to bring others to submission; it is an artifice of pride which abases itself to raise itself up; and although it is transformed in a thousand ways, it is never better disguised and more capable of deceiving than when it hides behind the face of humility.'

It is no doubt useful and even necessary to recognise that the ability to deceive, to dissimulate, to manipulate, to lie, is inherent in the human condition as the philosopher suggests, considering himself, for his part, a brother to his wolf. But it seems to me just as important, if not more so, to know, from a point of view not so much anthropological as historical, that this hardly laudable ability experienced an unprecedentedly significant development at a particular moment in the evolution of human society in which the habitus of the civilised person was set in place, characterised by a set of mechanisms of psychological self-control. It seems that among the primates it is only mankind that possesses a highly developed language. The tragedy is that this complex language has become an instrument allowing the art of cheating to be carried to its extremes. But what deserves special attention here is that, paradoxically, the sophistication and increasing complexity of this pernicious art have given rise at the same time to the birth of a certain literature that denounces this same art. Literature, then, appears as a mechanism that can thwart lies and dissimulation. Rousseau's work is in some way the culmination of this particular literary concern in the intellectual space of the Enlightenment.

DIARY EXTRACT 7

Mark Rowlands (who also quotes, if in passing, the passage from 'Karenin's Smile' that I have taken from *The Unbearable Lightness of Being*) wonders why he loved his wolf so much and why he suffers so painfully from his absence. The answer is simple: his life with Brenin has taught him that 'in some ancient part of my soul there still lived a wolf'. Here is a philosopher who is capable of remembering having been a wolf in the very distant past of humanity with which he identifies and, because of that, preserves the awareness of having a little of the wolf in his being today. The elegance of a philosophical reflection, the height of civilisation, shedding light on its own failing through the neon eye of a wolf who, himself, does not indulge in reflection … Civilisation in its highest realisation remembering the state before civilisation. That is a ray of hope, some grounds for comfort.

I remember a scene from Akira Kurosawa's remarkable film *Seven Samurai*. Among the seven warriors who dedicate themselves to the defence of the peasants' village against the faithless, lawless brigands there is one who is not quite like the rest. It is Kikuchiyo, unforgettably played by Toshiro Mifune. He claims to be descended from an honourable family of warriors, but all the signs mark him out from the others, from the long sword that he carries over his shoulders rather than on the hip at the side in the correct way, to his loose talk, not to mention his nonchalant gait and his constant shambling, swaggering movements. To be accepted by his fellows he has to undergo a test that will prove to them his qualities and talents as a samurai. Kambei (played by the admirable Takashi Shimura), the leader of the group, tells Katsushiro (the youngest of the recruited warriors) to strike Kikuchiyo hard when he comes through the door of the inn where they are waiting for him. A poor tramp berates Kambei, telling him that the candidate is blind drunk and that it isn't playing

'YOU ASK THAT I FORGET YOU? FEAR NOT, MY BELOVED.'

fair to attack him when he is like that. To which the head samurai, for whom Kikuchiyo in fact feels a great admiration, replies, 'A true samurai would know how to dodge the blow. He never drinks until he loses his wits.'

The blind drunk samurai receives a blow on the head, thus conclusively revealing his non-warrior origins ...

I don't know how many times I've seen *Seven Samurai* since my first viewing when I was still a high school student, I've lost count ... Each time I'm struck by the beauty of scenes like this one. And I especially like Kambei's firmly articulated reply: 'A true samurai, even in a state of drunkenness, never loses control of his body.' Spoken by a character who is the embodiment of moral integrity (Kambei is the first samurai to decide to take part in re-establishing the *res publica* of the peasants), this phrase had sounded in my ears as a lesson to be remembered.

The savage candidate has failed the test. But that won't prevent him from being accepted among the true civilised samurai. Kambei, the civilised philosopher, becomes attached to Kikuchiyo, the savage who secretly admires him. As for me, I like them both and I admire the filmmaker who created the two of them together, placing one opposite the other as if they were two complementary beings.

27
UNFAITHFUL—YET YEARNING FOR FIDELITY

AFTER MÉLODIE'S DEATH the habit of the daily walk was abandoned for a while. However, the need to take physical exercise together with our unfading memories of our dog meant that Michèle and I quite quickly rediscovered our enjoyment in taking a walk around where we lived, each time retracing one of the routes that we had taken with Mélodie.

It was May 2011. One Sunday morning, the weather mild and glorious, we let ourselves be tempted into going for a long walk, immersing ourselves in the profusion of light. It was one of those rare days that the inhabitants of Tokyo really appreciate, when the weather is dry, neither hot nor cold: a day without any climatic discomfort, midway between the oppressiveness of summer with its heat and humidity and winter sadly stripped of all adornment. Every street corner, every tree that signposted the route we used to follow, the cul de sacs where once, in complete safety, Mélodie would go chasing after a tennis ball, Philosophy Park with its sand-pit and swings, the memorial garden of Hyakkannon with its cherry trees, its maples and its Hundred Statuettes of the Merciful Goddess, all brought back the indelible presence of our dead dog, reminded us of the signs pointing to her singular existence. We took pleasure in every step, every stop we made, short or long, every laneway we ventured into, every play of light and shade created by the foliage quivering in the cooling breeze.

And so we had now arrived at the park of the Peaceful Forest. It was here that we used to shelter with Mélodie when it began to get hot in May or June: we were protected by giant trees majestically spreading their soft shade. It was here that we met our canine acquaintances. It was here that we'd met John, the huge pure-white golden retriever, Mélodie's father. We headed towards the shadiest part of the park, walking beside the 400-metre oval track, some early long distance runners there before us. Michèle pointed:

'Look over there! Isn't that a cousin of Mélodie's?'

Sure enough, it was a young, pure-white golden retriever being walked a little awkwardly by a woman in a green hat with a wide brim.

We went up to the dog, which careered in every direction, skipping and jumping for joy. Michèle said:

'He's still very young. How old is he?'

'Three months ... Today—it's his first outing after the vaccinations!'

At that moment a look of astonishment appeared on the face of the woman who was replying to Michèle's question while at the same time I recognised her as the woman I'd tripped up several months previously, the evening that Mélodie died.

'It's you!? This *is* a surprise! What a coincidence!'

As soon as I'd expressed my amazement I asked her what her dog's name was.

'Cello.'

'Cello. As in the instrument?'

'Yes, I like the cello. That's why …'

'Goodness!'

I explained to Michèle the whole mystery behind this unexpected encounter. Conversation then sprang up around Mélodie—I showed the woman with the green hat one of her photos that I'd kept on my iPhone—and about Cello, who was skipping around us, still with the same exuberance. It was a long time before we could bring ourselves to leave Cello, whose pure-white coat reminded us of Mélodie's at the same age. Seeing Cello we had the strange feeling of going back in time to the years when we were still young, very young, Michèle and I.

We wanted to make for the big avenue that separates the park from the administrative buildings that are part of the Ministry of Justice. Once the place where we'd meet other dogs, the straight avenue was deserted that morning. I remembered having taken a photo there of Michèle with Mélodie. Sitting on her hind legs next to Michèle, who was smiling that enchanting smile so typical of her, Mélodie too gave the impression that she was smiling …Words bubbled away in my head … I wanted to say something like: 'We lived with Mélodie for twelve years. How happy we were! And, Michèle, you and I, we've been together for thirty-five

'YOU ASK THAT I FORGET YOU? FEAR NOT, MY BELOVED.'

years ... thirty-five years, do you realise? So that makes thirty-five years that you've lived far from the land where you were born and grew up! ... Yes, I know I'm one of those people who values *deracination*. You know that I'm fond of the words of Hugues de Saint-Victor, quoted by Erich Auerbach and again by Edward Said: 'The man who finds his homeland agreeable is yet an innocent beginner; he for whom every land is like his native land is already strong; but perfect is he for whom the whole world is like a foreign country.' I would go so far as to say that deracination is even the condition that makes possible the notion of citizen that we both defend. But I realise that deracination is also a kind of wrench, a tearing away ... And that it hurts. You've been torn away from lots of things that were yours ... for me and because of me ... I know that it's been painful, that it still is, whether we like it or not ... I hope that having me by your side has been, is and will continue to be something that soothes this pain, even just a little ... This is all that I can wish for in the time remaining to us, which, I have no doubt, we'll spend together ...'

But I didn't.

My first book in French, *A Language from Another Place*, had been published a few months earlier. With the book the desire to write in French became incandescent. A number of subjects for a future book had me in their grip, if not obsessed me. And, if I remember correctly, it was on that day that I decided to write a book about Mélodie and weave into it a literary reflection about fidelity, this virtue that is at once human and yet scarcely human at all: human because man, by his destiny to be always already projected into an uncertain future, carries within him the prospect of fidelity, a desire for fidelity that is never extinguished; scarcely human because man—since he is a human, since he is no longer just an animal, since he has become fickle, as Don Alfonso teaches—by seizing this wonderful ability to transform himself, to construct himself continually, in short to give himself a story, could never be entirely faithful.

Oh, Mélodie! Have pity on me, I am just a poor wretched man who is unfaithful—but still I yearn for fidelity.

FINALE

28

'ALL THE ANIMALS ARE DEAD': THE AFTERLIFE OF MÉLODIE

I HAVE A cupboard—it has been made into a shrine, but it doesn't look like a shrine at all—that is now the quiet resting place of some unforgettable and unforgotten souls. In the cupboard there is a little box of lacquered wood for powdered tea that contains a tiny portion of my father's ashes that I had taken from his urn before it was placed in the grave. When I prepared this mortuary box, eighteen years ago now, I was brave enough to take a pinch of crumbled bones and taste them. Soon I think I'll do the same for Mélodie, whose urn I still keep close by me in the exact spot where her mattress lay. I shall get another box of lacquered wood and put in it some spoonfuls of powdered bone and a piece of shoulder blade or rib. The rest will be spread in the garden or somewhere else to return to the earth.

My father and Mélodie. As I've said, they are the two beings who appear most often in my dreams. They are dead,

FINALE

but they are here. The ancients kept the ashes of the deceased for forty-nine days and then they would part with them in order to forget the sadness and to bury it away in their memories. I haven't followed their teaching, because, while I understand the lesson, I wanted to go on living close to these two beings who, beyond the silence of death, continued to send me messages of encouragement. The man led me to the language with which and in which I write this book; the animal *who never lies* reinforced my loathing of sophistry and thus urged me to regard Literature still more as a vast and perilous attempt to expose words that lie. Man lies right up until death. But there are words, and arrangements of words, which, making this ultimate hypocrisy visible, escape at the very last from the lie. This text of Céline's invites us to discover such words and such arrangements of words:

> It's a fact, I still think of her, even now in this fever ... in the first place I can't tear myself away from anything, a memory, a person, so how would I tear myself away from a dog? ... I'm a virtuoso of fidelity ... fidelity and responsibility ... responsible for everything ... a disease ... anti-ungrateful ... the world is good to you! ... animals are innocent, even when they run wild like Bessy ... in a pack they shoot them ...
>
> I really loved her with her crazy escapades, I wouldn't have parted with her for all the gold in the world ...
> ... oh, she didn't complain, but I could tell ... strength all gone ... she slept beside my bed ... one morning she wanted to go out ... I wanted to lay her down in the straw ... right after daybreak ... she didn't like the place I put

'ALL THE ANIMALS ARE DEAD': THE AFTERLIFE OF MÉLODIE

her ... she wanted a different place ... on the cold side of the house, on the pebbles ... she lay down very prettily ... she began to rattle ... that was the end ... they'd told me, I didn't believe it ... but it was true ... she was pointed in the direction of her memory ... the place she had come from, the North, Denmark, her muzzle turned toward the north ... a faithful dog in a way, faithful to the woods of her escapades, Korsör up there ... faithful too to the awful life ... she didn't care for the woods of Meudon ... she died with two, three little rattles ... oh, very discreet ... practically no complaining ... and in a beautiful position, as though in mid-leap ... but on her side, felled, finished ... her nose toward the forests of the chase, up there where she came from, where she'd suffered ... God knows! ...

Oh, I've seen plenty of death agonies ... here ... there ... everywhere ... but none by far so beautiful, so discreet ... so faithful ... the trouble with men's death agonies is the song and dance ... a man is always on the stage...even the simplest of them ...[*]

We can marvel at the power and beauty of this text. Or rather the beauty that comes from the incredible power of the words, which take on the *cri de cœur* and the tears of a man going to pieces when faced with the death of his dog, a death that is at its most naked, its rawest, its truest. It was the author of *The Unbearable Lightness of Being* who, in *Encounter*, reminded me of and made me return to this magnificent passage from *Castle to Castle*. Bessy dies at Meudon from

---

[*] From Louis-Ferdinand Céline, *Castle to Castle*, trans. Ralph Manheim.

cancer, missing the North, Denmark, where 'for two, three hours ... this was one of her escapades ... wild in the animal world ... woods, meadows, rabbits, deer, ducks ...' It's the finest of all deaths: the death agony of the dog avoids all the song and dance that, necessarily and inevitably, accompanies man up until he dies ... Ceremony, staging, spectacle, spiel, bling, a whole layer of falseness, which prevents us from seeing what it is that's essential and ends up destroying it ...

Man tells lies even through the catastrophes that strew the earth with the dead in their thousands. For example, at the very time that an irremediable flaw of technology was revealed in the nuclear crisis at Fukushima, a crisis causing unspeakable suffering that in some respects is worse than death, man could not stop his lying. Faced with unbearable images and appalling risks, which at the least demand repentance and honesty on the part of those responsible for the disaster, we saw that man chose to carry on living with the lies, the humbug ...

We know that in France, as in Japan, an inconceivable number of dogs and cats are abandoned and euthanised every year. We also know that every day, in many countries, the world over, millions of animals raised on hormones are industrially slaughtered on a massive scale for the greater good. This unheard-of violence is undoubtedly the end result of the theory of animal-machines as it became established in the classical age. The extreme in terms of landscape, the endpoint presented to us by this radical disjunction between men and animals, is perhaps that of the contaminated zones of Fukushima where dogs, cats, cows, pigs, hens and other animals are dying in a state of intolerable abandonment and dereliction. It is indubitably one of the many, many consequences of the right claimed by modern man 'radically to separate humanity from animality' to use Lévi-Strauss's expression, while at the same time blinding ourselves to our primary nature as living beings.

While listening to Alain Finkielkraut's interview with Élisabeth de Fontenay for *Répliques* about her brilliant book *The Silence of Animals*, I remember hearing a magnificent passage by Paul Claudel, who refers to the death of all the animals in the world today:

> A cow is now a living laboratory, the pig is a product selected to provide a quantity of bacon conforming to the standard. The hen, adventurous and wandering, is incarcerated. Are they yet animals, creatures of God, brothers and sisters of man, signifiers of divine wisdom that we must treat with respect? What have we done to these poor servants of ours? Man has cruelly shown them the door. There are no longer any ties between them and us. And as for those that he has kept, he has taken their soul from them. They are machines, he has made the beast lower than a beast. And this is the fifth plague: all the animals are dead, not a one is still with man.

I often look at photos of animals taken at Fukushima. Some of them show extraordinarily acutely the suffering, the distress even, of a dog or a horse … This is the same distress, the same sadness I thought I saw a couple of times in the heart-rending look Mélodie gave me when I left her on her own for the whole day.

FINALE

I look for images of dogs in paintings. Mostly they are not particularly interesting. I don't like Oudry's dogs. They're painted as if they're automatons. I prefer Jacopo Bassano's *Two Hunting Dogs*. They're tied to a tree stump, and what they look is *sad*. The philosopher of *The Silence of Animals* refers to the great sadness in the expression of the horse that bears the knight in *Knight, Death and the Devil* by Albrecht Dürer. But I find his *Guard Dog*'s expression more moving.

Among all the images of dogs that I have looked at there is one that reaches out and clutches at me and won't let me go: Goya's painting *The Dog*, which is part of the famous 'Black Paintings' of the Quinta del Sordo. What exactly can we see in it? Almost nothing. All there is, in the lower part of the picture, is the tiny head of a dog who is buried beneath some darkish-coloured matter: sand or earth. The rest is just emptiness against an ochre background permeated by a kind of wash of diluted ink, tinged in places with a faint yellowish glimmer. To this I should really add that from the upper part of the painting, at the top right, there descends a dark, greenish, ghostly shadow like the disturbing symptom of an indefinable menace. The eye of the dog—wide open—oh, how it reminds me of Mélodie's!—is cast upwards. But since the pictorial space is bare, we do not know what it is looking at. The world is as if voided of its living matter. Claudel's phrase comes back to me: 'All the animals are dead'. Goya's dog is perhaps the last animal in the process of disappearing, of falling into nothingness. Man has already disappeared from the horizon. Has he deserted? Is he dead? Whatever the answer, in this desert, in this landscape of desolation that is the very negation of a landscape, there is no trace of man. And anyway, what man could live in such a void? What man would want to stay there? Can I speak, like Yves Bonnefoy, of 'an impulse, if only the mere hint of it, of compassion'? But, in this horror, in this denuded space that has now turned to dust, where nothing seems to breathe, isn't the emotion that seizes us rather one of anger? Even if—with that extraordinary eye—the painter, by according an attention both intense and delicate to this touchingly fragile animal, succeeds in making us share his own compassion …

In the extreme abstractness of its composition *The Dog* reveals a strange power, asking questions of all of those, wherever they may be, who look upon the at-once devastated and devastating landscape of post–11 March Fukushima, where, silently, the death agony of the animals seems to denounce the scandalous complicity of men mired in their own lies.

For me the afterlife of Mélodie will last a long time, a very long time.